LISTEN TO THE DRUM

Blackwolf Shares His Medicine

WHAT OTHERS ARE SAYING

My heart rejoices at the work of this talented sister and brother! The healing process revealed in these pages is a golden key that opens a new world...
I highly recommend reading and walking the Good Medicine of *Listen to the Drum*.
— Jamie Sams, author *Earth Medicine* and *Medicine Cards*

Blackwolf has woven life experiences, Native American teachings, and tools of transformation together in *Listen to the Drum*. This book will help you find your connection to the Creator and discover the truth that lies within you. *Listen to the Drum* resonates deeply in my heart. I highly recommend it.
— Walking Eagle, Spiritual Leader and Drug & Alcohol Counselor

Take time to read this book! Blackwolf has used intelligence and insight to bring authentic, ancient teachings into a useful modern context. His Give-away is a profound blessing to all who will take time to receive it.
— Steven McFadden, Director of Wisdom Conservancy,
Author of *Profiles in Wisdom* and *The Little Book of Native American Wisdom*

For centuries the beating of our Native Drum has joined our people together in harmony. Blackwolf captures our values and beliefs in *Listen to the Drum*.
— Kenneth R. Ninham, M.S.E./ CADC
(Oneida/Stockbrige-Munsee, Native American)

This is not a just book, it is a path. My hope is that readers will hug a tree, give their pain to the stone and water, and listen to their hearts. Touch, hear, smell, taste, see, know and be the teaching of *Listen to the Drum*.
— Phyllis Kasper, Ph.D., psychologist

Commune-A-Key Publishing
P.O. Box 58637
Salt Lake City, UT 84158
1-800-983-0600

Library of Congress Cataloging-in-Publication Data ·
Jones, Blackwolf, 1935-
    Listen to the drum: Blackwolf shares his medicine / by Blackwolf
    Jones and Gina Jones.
    p. cm.
    Includes bibliographical references and index.
    ISBN 1-881394-07-7 (pbk): $12.95
    1. Spiritual life.
    2. Healing.
    3. Indians of North America—Religion.
    4. Indians of North America—Medicine.
    I. Jones, Gina, 1960- .
    II. Title.
    BL624.J6473 1995   299'. 75—dc20
                            95-7778
                                CIP

Editorial: Caryn Summers and Nancy Lang
Cover Design: Lightbourne Images, Ashland, OR
Page Design: Quicksilver Productions, Mt. Shasta, CA

LISTEN TO THE DRUM

Blackwolf Shares His Medicine

Robert Blackwolf Jones, M.S., C.A.S.
and
Gina Jones

ommune-a-key
PUBLISHING

DEDICATION

This work is dedicated to the fellowship of Alcoholics Anonymous and its members. As co-authors, we are keenly aware that without our sobriety this book would not exist. The Yellow, Red, Black, and White races mix together in common cause and collective consciousness to form the Sacred Hoop of AA. As both Blackwolf and AA were born in the Spring of 1935 only weeks apart, it is fitting that this book be born while they celebrate their sixtieth year.

May the Twelve Steps of AA help to guide your moccasins as you walk down the Red Road of life. And may you echo the words of AA co-founder, Bill Wilson, and rest in "a quiet place in bright sunshine" with the healing of this book.

This book is not intended to elaborate on Native American teachings or ceremonies. For those seekers wanting more, you are directed to find an individual teacher or lodge.

This book is designed as a tool to assist the reader to eliminate unwanted memories, experiences and emotions, and replace them with positive responses. If you are currently being treated for an emotional or psychological disorder, or if your personal history suggests that you may need psychotherapeutic assistance, the authors recommend that you seek professional guidance before, during and after reading this book. If the reader experiences undesirable results, consequences or behaviors, the authors and publisher are not to be held responsible.

TABLE OF CONTENTS

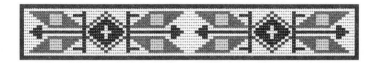

PREFACE

Blackwolf speaks:

Sister Cedar's familiar aroma coaxed me to awaken that early August morning. Only a few hours before the rhythmic waves of the Water Spirits lulled me to sleep. This cedar grove that edges Lake Michigan had announced its sacredness. As I breathed in its purity, having just left the Spirit World of dreams, I realized this was the moment for the asking. The asking for this book.

As with all important decisions made within traditional Indian culture, this decision was to be no different. The Spirit World would be consulted. So with deliberation I crawled out into twilight morning from my tent, and respectfully faced the East. I reached in and drew out some kinnikinnick[1] from my buckskin Medicine Bag, which was adorned with a tethered falcon claw. As I called the Eagle Spirit to come forth, I offered this mixture to push the day out from the night. I prayed to the Great Spirit on the wings of this Messenger. And I asked for this book.

I asked, "If I am to write this book, would the Spirit World validate my intention by gifting me with a feather from my Spirit Guide, the Eagle?" This would be the answer to my asking and I would honor the Spirit World's decision, feather or no feather.

---

[1] Kinnikinnick (meaning = much mixed) is a tobacco based mixture accompanied by other herbs, primarily: cedar, balsam fir, sweet grass, calamus root, sweet non-fern, sweet gale and mints. Other mixtures may include bear berry, sweet goldenrod, rose petals, sage, willow bark, red ooshier bark, sweet clover yarrow, and tobacco.

Moving to the East I traveled closer to the water's edge, my ears guided by the sound of the Water Spirits. Answering their call, my German shepherd, Maengun, and I neared their breaking waves. Grandmother Moon smiled down on us in her partial disclosure, and periodically touched the glimmer of the expansive lake. The Star People winked and twinkled as we traveled South down the sandy beach. I wondered if they had traveled this path from a distant time and now shared in this journey.

The passage I took was very much the same as the one I had discovered nearly sixty years ago. Nothing had changed. As a newborn focusing his eyes, my spirit had been comforted by the canopies of trees on an Ojibwa (Chippewa) reservation in Northern Wisconsin. The lacing of trees had been then, and remains now, a web of security as they meet the sky's horizon.

Continuing on my trail I let the water wash over my feet, just as my mother had bathed me in the Water Spirits of a spring fed glacial lake. It is all the same. These first impressions became my lifelong lens that I use to interpret reality. This "Way" was my way. This way was my only way to make sense of my existence. And through this constant reference, I tried to remain in harmony with the Universe.

Maengun and I moved up from the water's edge and West into the knee high saw grass that survived in the constant moving sands. With the first rays of the rising sun, I listened for the silence. For in the silence, all day and night creatures bow to Grandfather Sun, offering that moment to Him. The first rays penetrated the forest and the darkness retreated. As Earth Mother embraced the light energy, I offered my cupped hands and took communion by drinking in the first rays. And then I moved on to Brother Pine.

The pine. To the perch of the eagle, I headed. I had seen eagles using this particular tree to survey their hunting prospects. This pine, on the edge of the forest and the edge of the beach, supplied the eagle with a view of all. The dividing line of his world would determine my fate as well. As I reached the eighty-year-old pine, I again put down kinnikinnick. With my humble presentation, I asked Earth Mother to provide that which I sought and envisioned.

I searched the forest floor, remembering the ferns and moss that feathered my woodland bed as a child. From this Northern position I began. As I searched in circles, my memory replayed itself over and over, carrying a melody within my heart. The Anishinaabe[2] song. The song of principles, cycles, and rebirths. I thought of the turtles that still lay their eggs in the same place, in the same sand bank, on the same lake. I thought of hoops of endless circular motion. I thought of the teaching of the moon cycle, of birth and rebirth, illuminated in timeless predictability. I thought of the Four Directions that I had traveled. It is all a circle. A big circle. A winding circle. I searched. I searched under the decay at my feet that feeds the tree.

I stepped out of the forest. With no feather, I seriously questioned my vision of writing this book.

My dog companion looked at me, challenging my doubts and I began again my spiral exploration under Brother Pine. Maengun followed with satisfaction.

An hour later, empty handed, I concluded the Eagle-guide was not interested in my vision and venture. I stepped out of the forest onto the extensive shoreline to face this answer in the naked openness of the lake and sky. I looked to the shadows dancing beneath the clouds. They moved with Cousin Wind and left only a momentary trace of what they once were.

I looked down at my feet, thinking it was not meant to be. The answer had been given.

Yes. It had been given.

Yet... only a stone's throw from Brother Pine, I spotted some eagle plumage trapped by the sand, holding its need to puff up, safe from the prevailing Wind Spirits. In my tradition, the eagle plumage represents the innocent virtues of children. As if a child, I eagerly picked the feather up to feel its irresistible softness, and the seed of a new beginning was gently cradled in my hand. I saw my intentions declared pure.

---

2 Pronounced: A-ni-shi-NA-bae.

xv

Four steps later it was sealed. There at my feet rested the most magnificent white tail feather—the Eagle medicine feather.[3] The Spirit World had followed the current of intent. The answer had been given.

Gina speaks:

In the same month, August 1994, that the eagle feather was given to Blackwolf, a white buffalo was born in Wisconsin. Three hundred miles separated the unison of the buffalo and the eagle spirits. While the eagle gave its medicine feather at the top of Lake Michigan, the buffalo spirit presented itself near the bottom of this Great Water[4]. The Great Spirits had spoken.

Native American prophesy states that when the white bison returned, she would "unify the nations of the four colors—Yellow, Red, Black, and White." Thousands of people from across the United States have visited the calf named Miracle, to honor the Sacred birth. The calf is a reminder that people need to follow the sacred ways. The sacred pipe should come down from the mantle and become part of our experience rather than remain a decorated reminder of things past.

This book is about going back to the ways of old in order to become new. It is about returning to Self, embracing your pain, experiencing the healing, and thereby becoming. It is about the healer in you. For you are the giver. You are your own remedy.

You will receive techniques and awarenesses that will lead you on your journey. Obviously, you have already begun on the path that leads to the center of your being, or you wouldn't have picked up this book. Something in you asked for permission to look at this. To look at you.

Blackwolf, a healer himself, has given me the remedies and understandings he uses in his psychotherapy practice, where he special-

---

3 Known in Ojibwa tradition to be used in healing.

4 Michi-Gami (Michigan) means Great Water.

izes in the addictive disorders. As a teacher and writer, I have enjoyed shaping his insights into the book that is now in your hands, to offer you the teachings of many thousands of years of living. It is as though he had offered me clay to sculpt with, and it is my privilege and honor to be asked to present it to you.

As you read, you will be hearing two voices harmonizing one message. To be sure, it is Blackwolf's steady beat that has given this book its life. It is his understanding that he offers first to me, then I to you.

Isn't that the way of all things permanent? All life continues, as long as there is someone, or something, to receive its energy, its meaning, its quest for continuation. We offer you these gifts. We offer you the truth that has been left in the sieve of life.

There are times in life when you are certain of what you need to do. Doors begin to open and the truth is spoken without you ever knowing you knew. That is how it is with this venture. I dipped my paint brush in Blackwolf's colorful palette and the beauty of Old Age wisdom effortlessly emerged from each touch of my brush. Blackwolf and I are grateful for this opportunity to share this certainty, this life-art, with you.

We come together to give to you the gifts given to us by many people. You will hear Blackwolf's voice echo the "Old Age" tribal wisdom. You will also hear the voices of many people, in both our lives, who have spoken

Please listen to their wisdom, to their truth.

As the birth of the white bison brings people together, it is our hope that these words will gift you into becoming a vital participant in making the prophesy of old come true. May the "Miracle" healing of all nations begin and the unification of all people become a reality.

Heal and be healed.

ACKNOWLEDGMENTS

Listen to the Drum: Blackwolf Shares his Medicine has been a WE project from conception to birth. Therefore, we would like to thank the following people for their gifts along the way:

~ To my father for teaching me how to make wise decisions.

~ To my mother for teaching me how to be happy and joyous.

~ To my sister for teaching me how to play.

~ To my grandfather for teaching me how to be a good friend.

~ To my grandmother for teaching me how to be honest with the loud candy dish lid.

~ To my friend, Aught, for teaching me how to glide the stressful currents of life.

~ To my friend, Jim, for putting me up when I was down.

~ To my German Shepherd for investigating every scent in the woods.

~ A Special thank you to "Moccasin Mike" Bostoni for teaching me the Indian ways.

-Blackwolf-

~ To Mom for your foresight and your pride of our heritage.

~ To Dad for your insight and your openness to the wonder of the Universe.

~ To my Grandparents for helping me fill my Medicine Bag.

~ To my sister, my friend, for giving and sharing.

~ To my brothers for your continuous loving support.

~ And to my friend Lori, who is my teacher of true selflessness and fun.

-Gina-

Together we wish to offer our gratitude:

~ To our children, for your support, patience, and love and for holding Earth Mother and Sky Father in respect.

~ To Caryn Summers, for believing in Blackwolf's message and gently guiding our words. Your soft eye truly blessed this project from beginning to end.

~ To Nancy Lang, your hard eye polished while your soft touch took great care of our words.

~ Migwetch Megiziquay (Eagle Woman) for teaching us in your lodge.

~ Gitchi Migwetch to all Native American tribes, lodges, and people for all you have given and taught us. We beg your forgiveness for our limited understanding of the ways.

~ And to Gitchi Manidoo for endorsing this book by sending a sacred Eagle Feather.

INTRODUCTION

FROM PAIN TO CHANGE

Prepare for a journey within
where mystery unravels into Self.
This is where the listening must begin.
In order to plug into the spiritual dimension,
you must first reconnect to your own essence,
to where your attachment to the Mother
of this physical dimension was conceived.

That is where I begin.

In the spring of 1935, a Medicine Man of the sacred Midewinin Eagle Lodge came to see an old spirit in a new body. As Moccasin Mike came through the woods to the home where the child slept, he saw a black wolf. A wolf never reported seen before nor since that day. A wolf of mystery. The Mother dimension recognized me in this way.

I am called Muka-day-way-gun.
I am Blackwolf.

The visitation of my brother wolf would be the first of many similar connections to the Spirit World, reinforcing my Primary Essence. It wasn't long before Mike came to visit from across the lake in his row boat and witnessed still another interesting sight. As he was beaching the boat by our shoreline, he noticed me, a toddler, pulling on a pine snake's tail. As the snake tried to get away, I would pull him back. Mike told me that he sat in his boat and watched this continue for a long time, until I finally became disinterested in the game and let the snake go. I had been harnessed with a rope around my body and tied to a tree so as not to be able to enter the lake and drown. I was restrained quite often as a child and this feeling of constriction permeated my adulthood. Ironically, the internal harnesses I have struggled against have been of my own making.

And in two worlds, I have struggled.

The Indian world of the reservation in Northwestern Wisconsin and the non-Indian world of Southeastern Wisconsin became a constant teeter-totter for me. For the first eighteen years of my life, I was in continual transition from the reservation to the city and back again. Constantly searching for the values and the energy of the other world, I became nomadic, roaming the United States, Canada, and Europe. From big cities to back woods, from the fast lane to the slow, I merged in and out of the "where-do-I-belong?" traffic.

My father abused alcohol, and was physically and verbally abusive. Having been orphaned, he had never been taught how to be warm and close. The memories of hugs and kisses were not to be mine.

I saw life as a very hostile place and developed a lot of anger and anxiety. By high school and college, I found an outlet for this anger playing football and boxing. In fact, at one time, I had seriously considered professional boxing. It would be better to inflict my own pain and get paid for it.

Like my father, I, too, became an alcoholic, medicating myself with alcohol and drugs for twenty years. Assaulting myself with fists of delusion and internal agony, I learned how to beat myself up very well. The harder I punched, the further I retreated from myself, from life, from it all. I became so far distanced from my Self that I was functioning on the most superficial level of being human. Living in the physical realm had become nearly impossible. Emotion was completely numbed with thick, alcoholic escape. I experienced the absence of Self and nearly closed the door to any possibility of connecting to the spiritual realm.

But the door was pushed wide open by the Wind Spirits. I begged to be let back into this world after traveling through a spiritual maelstrom of the darkest, coldest, emptiest Absence.

As the result of this spiritual experience, I entered sobriety on March 30, 1977 at 6:30 P.M. and have been sober to this day. Since that moment of change my life has taken a new direction, primarily due to Native American healing techniques, many of which I will share with you in the following pages. This ancient set of remedies designed to change our way of thinking, feelings and actions, have survived thousands of years of medical 'progress,' because they work for us.

My story is not unlike others. Yet it is unique all the same. Just as your life story is uniquely you. Brother snake continues to teach me about myself, begging me to let go of the illusionary fight for life, to yield and embrace the joy of living. I am fortunate to have escaped the bondage I had imposed on myself.

What is your struggle? What is your conflict? What intrapsychic warfare do you experience? What are your chains? Whatever they are, I invite you to let go of your snake's tail. Soon you will ride the currents of life, just as the eagle tips its wing to feel the wonder of the sky.

PART ONE

LISTEN TO THE SILENCE

I invite you to stop...and listen.
I encourage you to attend...and listen.
I urge you to experience.

And listen.

THE WINDS OF CHANGE

"If we always do what we've always done,
we'll always get what we've always got.
And if nothing changes...
nothing changes."

Alcoholics Anonymous

RECOGNIZING CHANGE

All too often we can't see that something needs to be changed, that something is weighing us down. Many of us do not realize that we carry so much baggage with us. It is a sign of health when we begin to become aware of our problems and start to identify our symptoms.

In Indian, we say, "How would a fish know it's in water?" The only way a fish would know it's in water is if it were taken out of water. Many of us have experienced some degree of depression, anxiety or other emotional problems. Often, we were unaware of the affliction as it was happening within us. However, once our problems dissipated, we realized just how encumbered we had been. We fight the reality of our conditions and their remedy, just as a fish fights for air that is so obviously plentiful.

Not long ago I hiked the Greenstone Trail, the backbone of Isle Royale, an International Biosphere Reserve on Lake Superior. Those fifty miles of trail taught me more about myself than sitting in fifty hours of therapy. Why? Because it was experiential.

When I shed my pack after hiking up and down the rugged Isle terrain, I felt as though I were floating. So light. So easily me. So open to any possible experience asked of me. Likewise, our burdens once lifted, allow us the freedom to be what we need to be. The majority of our mental health issues are formed by negative life experiences. This is a critical factor, because it usually takes other experiential events to diminish or extinguish our original experiences. Once you have been able to identity your beast of burden, I will show you, experientially, how to shed its weight and remove its chains.

NOW has been given to you to do this act of honesty and self-appraisal.

Take the time you need, NOW, to give yourself the gift that the Universe is offering. Feel the weight of your pain and hear the suffering inside your silence.

Have you identified your pain? Can you embrace its existence? Are you willing to acknowledge that it takes a thorn to remove a thorn? For those of you who are being honest with yourselves, and who are finding courage inside the fear, I applaud your first step towards achieving health and meaning in life.

What you will read ahead will guide you into an experiential way of being. You will experience change. Become change. Crave for even greater change. Contrary to the assumption that change is uncomfortable, I contend that change, embraced in its entirety, is the silk of our cocoon. Change is the silk of our own making, the garments we wear to the wedding of Self and the Spirit World. There will always be some pull. You will either be pulled into greater pain, or you can acquiesce to the gravity of change and connect to the Mother of the Spiritual World.

To change your external world circumstance, I invite you to change your internal world circumstance. Spin your silk in the color you have chosen as uniquely you, and become your seventh direction[1]. The silk that binds you to the center, your essence, is your umbilical cord to Life.

LISTEN TO THE VIBRATIONS OF NATURE

Change came to my reservation in the Forties. But Moccasin Mike, from across the lake, remained constant for me. I recall a time when he sat saddle-less on Archie, his white horse. His lower left leg followed the horse's contour and a black and white canvas tennis shoe was fit snugly onto his self-crafted wooden leg. It wasn't really a leg, it was more a peg, a sturdy, straight, dependable wooden peg-leg. I remember his pant leg pulled high, his sock held up with a few well placed silver thumb tacks on the weathered wood. I wanted to laugh at the comical way the thumb tacks looked, but as a young boy, I looked at it straight-faced. Moccasin Mike lost his leg during a logging accident in the 1800's. The missing leg reminded me to respect the experience and wisdom of my elders.

From his horse, Mike spoke these words to me, "To be Indian is to hug a tree." His focus was never negative, never about his leg, never about his loss. Instead, he would talk about the way of living.

Fifty years later, I understood what he meant. Mike wanted me to learn from the tree and to appreciate its gifts, just as he appreciated the gift of his wooden leg.

The tree has lessons for us to learn. Lessons which apply to our own healing. To learn the lessons, we must look beyond the tree's apparent 'limits'. We must look to the invisible connections that are as real as the bark we peel from the tree. Look beyond the branches' tips which reach out to honor and embrace Sky Father. Look into

---

[1] The seventh direction on the Native American Medicine Wheel represents your Self. Focus upon this direction reveals the changes one must go through to become what one is meant to become.

Earth Mother, where the roots penetrate and wait for the gift of nour-ishment. From both the visible and invisible, the sap flows, manifest-ing life force. Creator energy cycles itself. The channel for it all is visible. The Spirit World has given us the opportunity to learn from this truth. The tree trunk is the connector of energy between Heaven and Earth. The Spirit World communicates through vibrations.

Not long ago, I had an attorney as a client. He was brilliant, yet his intelligence had distanced him from the beating of his heart. This was his sixth or seventh treatment. One day after a group session where we all listened to him devalue the idea of the Spirit World, I said, "I'm giving you an assignment. I want you to go outside and find yourself an oak tree. A good, big one. And give it a hug. I want you to feel the energy of the Universe. Feel the energy of the Creator."

Looking at me like I was not playing with a full deck of cards, he said, "Can I wait till dark?"

I smile when I think of his response. It is very natural for many. Many of us have become so removed from our natural world, that the idea of hugging a tree is embarrassing. Yet, determined to do well and motivated to heal himself, my client decided to be a good student and do what was asked of him. Although he did wait until dark, he hugged a tree. He came down from his lofty high horse and dared to ride the horse of Moccasin Mike. The white horse of respect. Alone, he was able to close his eyes on himself. Without the threat of judgment this man allowed himself to listen, perhaps for the first time in his life, to the silence begging to be heard. Inside that moment, he experienced tree vibrations. The vibrations of the Great Mystery. The attorney opened himself to the connection of the invisible and the visible. He allowed nature to activate his spirituality! The Now he experienced was the springboard to his experiential healing. The vibrations of nature soothed his pain.

I saw him a while ago and the extent of this event is remarkable. His whole life has changed. He maintains a spiritual consciousness and hugs trees whenever he feels the need for connection to the Spirit World. Even during the day.

In Indian all vibrations are sacred, the spirits are conduits to the energy flow, like the hummingbird that hitchhikes on the back of a migrating goose. The Spirit World and the physical world work together in harmony, just as physical laws of nature work together.

So right now I urge you to select a tree large enough to get a firm, hugging grip. With soft eyes and silken touch, allow the connection to happen, as the attorney did. Ask the tree to strengthen you. Feel the vibrations and allow your energy vibrations to connect to the Spirit World. And like Mike, thank the tree for sharing its energy. This will be the beginning of experiencing the healing.

TREES, CYCLES, REJUVENATION

What lesson did you learn from Brother tree? Have you recognized the song of life it sings through its needles, leaves and boughs? Trees have much to say if we listen.

A tree can not flee the stresses of life. It must learn to adapt or perish. It roots itself deeply down into the earth as an infant. It learns to flourish where it is planted. If unencumbered, it grows up "straight as a stick." If it encounters obstacles, it exercises flexibility and adjusts to limited sunlight by curving upward to maintain balance while seeking nourishment.

Become determined in your pursuit of psychological, mental, spiritual, and emotional nourishment. Reach down into Earth Mother and become flexible enough to bend, but not break, as you reach up to Sky Father.

Reserve the right to change your mind about anything at anytime, because life variables are in constant change. Stay in the Now, be strong in the present. The willow and the mighty oak stand side by side in the forest. Along comes a wind storm and which remains? The willow remains, because it is flexible enough to yield to life tensions. This tree knows its limits and boundaries well, that it needs to be rooted and flexible simultaneously, constantly centered and balanced.

It moves and grows in its own curve. This may be its greatest teaching to us.

Trees are a renewable resource because they continue to recycle themselves. If you have ever cut a maple tree down, you will know its roots are programmed to reproduce itself many times. It may well spring up ten to twenty replacement shoots. If the top of a spruce or pine tree is severed, it will retaliate with a double effort and grow two heads. How can you compensate for the injuries inflicted upon you? What can you learn from this determination for self preservation?

I know a woman who was the victim of great abuse in her youth. She had many hurdles to overcome, many tears to shed. Yet, deep inside her Self preservation flowed. She allowed herself to experience the pain, flow with the wind, and is now becoming as she was meant to be.

When Fall comes, trees display their carnival-color-robes like an Indian blanket, and they teach us to yield to death and die gracefully. Death is the ultimate life experience. I recently returned from the Fall deer hunt, and I saw the autumn leaves dropping from the forest trees. They were being freed from their branches by the Wind Spirits of change. In rich color regalia, they danced lightly in graceful descent to blend with Sister Water and Mother Soil to form a fertile mix for Infant Seeds. Can you see how the acceptance of death compliments the prior hunger for survival? That death is the survival of our spirit?

When the tree finally lays down for its final rest, it converts itself to fodder and cuddles the vulnerable seedling that needs a mother's womb to flourish. This newborn will grow, and its bark and roots will gift us with the cradle board, the bow, the campfire, and many kinds of medicine. The outer wood of Sister Cedar provides material for the bow, and the fibers of her inner bark provide the bowstring. Her boughs become a mattress or a medicinal tea[2]. All are gifts of the

---

[2] Cedar is also used in many spiritual ceremonies providing a channel to the Spirit World.

cycle, and you are part of this cycle, as well. You are a gift from the Spirit World.

LESSONS FROM EARTH MOTHER

When you were hugging your tree, did you notice that you were not alone? When the trees sang to you, were they accompanied by a squirrel or a bird? Did you wonder what lessons the animals have to teach us?

The mouse teaches us concentration and focus, but not to be overcome with preoccupation, for then he becomes distracted and vulnerable to the hawk's hunt. Find the balance of focus in your life. Look up from time to time or you may miss the most important lesson of all. The mouse teaches us a lesson of soft and hard focus.

Right now, look at something wherever you are. Focus on it with a hard eye. Stay with it for awhile. Intensify your concentration. Notice the limits you place on yourself. Notice the tension. Now, allow your eyes to relax, notice your peripheral vision. Notice the calming inside you. Notice how you can see more, do more, be more. This is the soft focus of the Spirit World. This is the focus that teaches many lessons, for you are able to see beyond your nose. This is the soft focus of change. Look to Earth Mother with a hard eye to participate as you must, but also, look with a soft eye to see what is about you.

My name sake, the wolf, teaches us endurance, strategic planning and perseverance. A wolf can run like the wind or be as still as a stone. There is a time for us to be quiet and centered like the stone and a time for us to actively pursue our aspirations and predetermined goals. First we need to meditate to gain strength to fill our energy reservoir, just as the wolf effectively uses life's energies. This inherent wisdom is handed down to your pet dog as he knows how to rest well, breathe deeply while resting, stretch upon wakening and run with effortless propulsion. This is how to enjoy life in rest and motion with the collection and release of energies.

Beavers teach of purpose. Through endless chewing and gnawing, trees fall, dams and canals are built, forests are changed forever. See the comfort inside the beaver's lodge. Find the hidden channels that extend to forest edge. Hear the slap of his tail that warns of danger. Discover that Brother Beaver gives up his safety in order to save others. While the beavers have engineered both their home and transportation, the aging of the forest is accelerated and rich land is left behind. Look to see what you can chew on. Plan your own acceleration of change and growth. Create your own home and channel to the Spirit World.

Think of other animals. What are they known for? What are their lessons? Every animal, bird, fish and bug has a lesson to teach, just as every human being has something important to tell. It is time to listen and learn from them.

Look to what is not visible. What we see is really not what we see.

I am reminded of a time when my son and I were at a boat landing at Indian Lake[3]. It was a cold November day, and Joel decided to skip a stone.

Expecting to see the stone skip across the lake and sink beneath its waters, it instead simply skipped and stopped. Apparently floating, the stone remained on top of the water. But how could that be? Stones don't float.

I decided to skip my own stone over the water. The skipping of the stones turned into sheer skidding. All of my stones remained on top of the water, as well.

We couldn't believe our eyes. So we decided to get close to the water's edge to see what could be causing this improbable phenom-

---

[3] Indian Lake is the lake where I grew up.

enon. We looked into the water and saw nothing out of the ordinary. We could still see the sand on the bottom, the movement of the water. But our eyes would never have been able to show us the truth. It was only when we touched the water that we felt the very beginning stage of ice formation. This was the sheerest glass I have ever seen, allowing the lake to hold the stones upon its surface.

What we saw, was not what we saw.

Sometimes a feeling is required in order to fully understand the truth. I ask you to feel the connections which are presented. If you simply look, you will only see some of the connections, not all. Practice soft focus and develop presence. Become aware of your surroundings at all times.

My grandfather taught me to honor natural laws. As a small boy, I helped him plant white pine seedlings in a decaying log. Death would give to Life, he told me. Grandpa told me to take my small bucket and fill it from the creek to moisten the transplants. Within his view, I did as I was instructed. But when I returned to where our seedlings awaited, he told me to pour the water back into the creek rather than pour it on the seedlings. When I asked why, he told me I hadn't extracted the water in the same direction the current was going, that I had held my bucket against the current. I had to put the water back into the creek and once again fill my bucket, this time going with the current.

Grandpa understood the energies of the Universe and that we must not interfere with their motion or purpose. Nature is an organic whole. The Indian does not try to conquer nature like the non-Indian. The Indian flows with nature.

What matters here, and will be addressed in the pages ahead, is that your energy, your life, be it negative or positive, does matter. Your emotions, your perceptions ride their own waves of energy.

Think of a time when you entered a room where two people were arguing. Without seeing or hearing them, you could feel the tension in the room. The invisible became observable. You are responsible for your own energy and what eventually takes place with it. The Universe *does* notice. Your efforts *are* felt. Your pain *can* interfere with the healing process of others. Once you understand how to blend the physical and Spiritual world, your negative energy can be released and the purification process can begin. You can develop a positive focus out the ashes of your own Phoenix. The adversity of pain that speeds your pulse can fuel a rebirth of joy. Allow the fire that now consumes you to ignite a new beginning.

Our emotions and perceptions are constantly in flux, changing, being transformed. Joy is our pain turned upside down, inside out. It is time for us to appreciate the dichotomy and to flow with the current of change. If we remain connected to our life source, all of life is bearable. All of life is necessary. Within each present we experience, we become more of who we need to be. Every experience that we have had, therefore, has a kernel of nourishment for us to partake. Use your soft eye and see inside the nourishment which direction you crave. Develop your own presence.

It is your responsibility and your obligation, to your Self and the Spirit World, to become aware of all that is you. Awareness, listening to your own pain, is the initial step to healing.

The silence between the beats is where you hold hands with the invisible. Turn your wing tips into the current of the invisible and feel the possibilities that the winds of change can bring to you.

LISTEN

This book is about listening at the deepest level. It is about learning to listen to yourself, to your world, and ultimately to your silence.

The results of true listening are authentic, far-reaching and profound, and always within simple awareness. Native American traditions teach how to hear with open ears. As we learn to tune in and hear the silence, we are able to truly listen. Now is for the listening experience. The effects today will matter five years from now, fifty years from now and all the nows beyond now. Now is for you to be healed.

Perhaps the greatest distinction between the Indian and non-Indian culture is the degree of proficiency in the art of listening to the Drum. Listening to the drum requires you to be present in the now. The space of silence between the beats, is where one listens in respect. I invite you to put your ear to the pulse, to the drum of creation, and listen to the heartbeat of the Universe.

Smell the scent of the rose-flower which hints of the rose-plant from which it was taken. The perfume squeezed from the flower connects you to its essence, its source. We can know the Creator in a similar encounter. When we stop, pay attention and sniff the scent around us, we can connect to the essence of Life.

Make no mistake. A connection is needed. An experience is required. Stop and pay attention to the now, to the silence, and experience.

People try to get to the Spirit World mentally. You can't get there from there. A finite mind can't understand an infinite being. In fact, the longest distance in the Universe is from the head to the heart. You must know the Spirit World through experience. Smell the flower, listen to the birds sing the symphony of the Universe, and embrace the Spirit World with joy and exhilaration.

SPIRIT / MATTER: DEATH / LIFE

Native American traditions recognize that the Spirit World is senior to the physical world. As in the way of all things, the cycle of life whispers this supremacy. As you are listening to this truth, experiencing the rose, it is easy to recognize that the Spirit World is parent to all physical existence, giving birth to the physical dimension.

In Native American understanding, a baby is an old-spirit in a new body, rather than a body with a new spirit. Once we acknowledge that we are spirits with bodies rather than bodies with spirits, there is greater opportunity for connection. Inside this scent of truth, our old thoughts reverse. It is as though we have worn clothes of truth inside out, and are now able to wear them as they were meant to be.

Spirit is the essence and source of breath, the vehicle for creative connections to occur within. Our spirit is connected to our Mother World by an invisible umbilical cord from which our breath emanates. In other words, you are breathed by the Great Spirit. You do not breathe yourself. When the Great Spirit discontinues to breathe us, we return back through the tunnel to the Spirit World that we originated from. Death is the giving back of breath to the One Breath of Life.

It is the silent voice of this life energy that sustains us. This cord connects our spiritual and ordinary realms. Each vibration offers silent revelation.

The Spirit World is the Parent of this physical dimension and Universe. The hard and soft, the female and male, nurturance and sustenance are born of the Spirit World. Our complete Parent is honored as separate images. Sky Father and Earth Mother each reveal distinct aspects of the Great Spirit. Sky Father asks us to look up to what was and will be again. Earth Mother asks us to connect to what is now. Keep an eye on each dimension. While you are here, connect to Earth Mother. Your life experience requires this. If you want to influence your life experience, you need to appeal to the Mother of the child. The harmony we sing with Her occurs in the space of silence. And the song we sing is the song of experience.

Mother is the source of nourishment. Peace, serenity, joy and bliss are the fruits of Her blessing. As we ground ourselves and achieve balance within our center of being, we connect to Earth Mother whose heart vibrates with the soothing energies of the Spirit World. Some use Jesus as a path to connection. Others use Buddha, Krishna, or Mohammed. Native Americans use the eagle feather, sacred pipe, sage, sweet-grass, cedar, and kinnikinnick as a way to connect the Spirit World with the physical realm. It is about blending. About attending. About experiencing. All paths are beneficial, if they accomplish the coupling of spiritual and physical worlds.

The Feather

I gently picked up the white tail feather by its bottom shaft. My heart raced with excitement, as I knew the Spirit World found my intent pure. As my thumb rolled its handle across the pads of my fingertips, the feather turned with easy lightness. My spirit, too, soared with the gift I now held. Back and forth I rolled it, over and over it turned. "The feather is here. It will be so. The book will become," I repeated. "Migwetch[4]."

Continuing my play, the feather met the air without resistance. It moved without effort. It blended with Cousin Wind. "It loves the air," I observed, and saw its connection to the invisible. The feather's love of the invisible gave the feather its power, gave me strength.

I sat down in the sand and instinctively began straightening the feather's individual fibers, smoothing them to come together at the tip. "There would be much to do. Much to plan. Much to say," I thought now of the book. Each barb touched the one next to it with gentle respect, the need for each other apparent. I marveled how all became one. I realized this white tail feather was

---

[4] Migwetch is pronounced: ME-gwich and means thank you.

gifted from under all the rest of Brother Eagle's plumage. It had supported and given direction to them all. I knew then that this endeavor would become WE, that this magnificent medicine feather would help me give direction to others. This feather would heal. I said, "Migwetch."

Slightly curved, I noticed how the hollow shaft held the feather's secret. This passageway was the conduit to both dimensions. It was the support, the channel. I knew it would also be my channel as I held it in my hands. I needed to listen to its silence. I needed to hear its stories.

Separating the fibers, I noticed the space between. Each opening had a story to tell, for it had flown on the winds, touched the currents of cold and heat, of cloud and sun. It had seen it all. I stopped and wondered what the world looked like from Feather's point of view. What injury had caused the frayed edges? What splendor did Feather see? What music did Feather hear? What invisible did Feather touch?

In the warm rays of Grandfather Sun, holding this gift of Brother Eagle, I glimpsed the scene, I heard the echo of the song, I touched the shadow of the Great Spirit. It spilled out as a tear, and I said, "Migwetch."

I thought of returning to camp, as Grandfather Sun was growing hot. Maengun rested at my feet and twitched his ears as the flies tried to sit on him. Making circles with my wrists, Feather pulled in

Cousin Wind from all directions and coaxed the flies to leave my dog alone. I closed my eyes, continuing to fan Feather and accept the same cool gift of Cousin Wind. As it touched my face, I asked the Four Directions to guide me. I asked the Great Spirit to teach me. I asked the Eagle to help me fly alongside him.

Brushing off the sand and holding Feather high, I said, "Ah ho, Migwetch."

DIFFERENCES / UNIQUENESS

We are all connected to the Universe, and we are all expected to give and take from its delicate balance and abundance. We are able to see the place for us. Yet, we are also unique. It is our weaknesses and shortcomings, as well as our strengths, that make us unique and distinguish us from others.

Consider a blade of grass. Please, go choose a blade from the many. Get acquainted with it and befriend your green-relative. Come to realize that this is the only blade of grass in the Universe exactly like it. Recognize that there never was, nor ever will be, another blade exactly like this one. Come to realize your uniqueness and understand that the Universe has chosen you to exist out of an infinite number of options.

Compare how Indians and non-Indians respond to hungry mosquitoes. An Indian will usually let a mosquito have its fill and then allow it to go on to satisfy its destiny; or, they might brush them off with a long soft stroke of their hand. Compare this to a non-Indian who slaps himself silly trying to get rid of the "pest." Scientists acknowledge that when all the bugs and insects die, people will have about three months to live, for there will be no oxygen. Nature will cease to be (including trees). When a bug dies, the Universe takes note, as all of nature is dependent upon one another.

The words of Chief Seattle speak to this truth, "Man did not weave the web of life, he is merely a strand in it. Whatever he does to the web, he does to himself." Indeed, every time I hear one of those bug zappers go 'zizz', my heart shudders for the toll it takes on the balance of a delicate web.

In a nearby town, there is a billboard sponsored by a local church which reads, "Human life is sacred." I would revise that to read, "All *Life* is sacred; *WE* are all related." It is time to climb down from the lonely pedestal we have created for ourselves and recognize our place alongside our fellow inhabitants. "Mitakuye-Oyasin" means, "We are all related." It goes beyond the boundaries of the human race.

SPIRIT CONNECTION

The primal tribes of the world understood that invisible spirits manifested themselves in the solid world in the forms of water, air, sun, stars, moon, wood, rock, animals, etc. They were aware, connected, and invested in the invisible realms. They appealed to Sun Gods to deliver nurturing energies and they prayed to Water Gods to deliver life-giving energies from thunder-bird clouds onto their parched lands.

Today people have distanced themselves from the invisible Spirit World our ancestors knew and depended upon. This has caused a void which is being filled with pollution and the disintegration of the food chain in the balance of nature. All of this is justified as 'progress' and the wonderful world of technology.

This detachment from spirit emphasizes the 'ME' of the non-Indian world, as opposed to the 'WE' of Indian philosophy. Many deny the physical world's relationship to its Parent—the energy of the invisible Spirit World.

It is easy to recognize the connection of matter to the visible. Unfortunately, it is difficult for many to see the same connection of energy to the invisible. And harder still, to see the umbilical cord that ties the visible and invisible together.

Native American tradition understands that we share our breath with all of the visible: the deer, bear, hawk, snake, tree, and shark. It is the Wind Spirits that move the breath from west to east, mingling each breath with the Source of all life. I challenge you to see that we also share our breath with the Spirit World. The smoking of the sacred pipe is a Native American tradition of making the invisible—visible. The smoke becomes the visionary instrument, illuminating the mingling.

Can you see that you and I share the same breath and that by doing so, we actually become one with each other?

It takes the soft eye of silk to allow this openness to the Spirit World to occur. Likewise, it takes the hard eye of stone, to see and be in the physical world. The stone contains the shell of the exterior physical world, just as a nut has its shell. The internal energy of the Spirit World, however, is always present and ready to give the nurturance needed to live.

If I asked you to draw the moon right now, what would it look like? Many would draw the night moon as circular, or partially crescent, and shining. And that is fine. However, ponder the truth of the moon as it reflects upon the waters. The shimmering light moving with the waves is different, but just as real. So is the day moon, although it is invisible during the sun's time, it is just as real as the nighttime sky view that everyone accepts.

So right now, see with day-moon awareness and move with the waves of sparkling waters. Try to listen to the silence of the unseen, and hear the moving vibrations of the Spirit World.

It is here, in the Great Mystery of Life, that you need to appeal for change. Listen to the silence and experience Earth Mother. Celebrate your uniqueness and connect to all of life. With soft eye, see the cord that connects the invisible Spirit World to Earth Mother. The wise person appeals to the mysterious silence of the Spirit World to make significant change within the physical world.

PREPARE

I heard the song of whippoorwill
I sang it in my heart.
I wondered why it sang at night
the song of day's new start?

Your decision to continue suggests that you are recognizing, at some level, the truths that Native American people have embraced for centuries. You are understanding that the invisible exists, that your world is full of vibrations. You have come to the bed of silence where your Primary Essence rests. Hear the song of letting go, of directing your Self, of giving what you must to this journey. Prepare for the pain. Prepare for the joy, for they are both your companions. Prepare for a new day.

LET GO

Perhaps you have already begun on your path of change and are experiencing the pain of previous pains, as you open the cover to the book of your own life. The cover, which up to now, had been carefully sealed up. Like the leaves of a head of lettuce, you are beginning to peel back one blemished leaf at a time, to reveal the you of quiet peace. Hidden beneath your polished presentation to the world, your injuries have been waiting for you to acknowledge their existence. It is time to view your injuries and feel your bruises. Through this experiential process, we become real. We really become. We see through naked openness, for the goal of life is to meet death transparently.

I would imagine there is a kind of anticipation or even a celebration taking place inside you. Up to now, you may have stood in line to receive healings from other people, groups, or books. Hands held out, you hoped for the remedy. For hope is how we cling to sanity.

I say: let go.

Dare to feel the insanity. Paradoxically, this frees our sanity. There is nothing without the experience. Without experiencing each pain, our coping mechanisms crumble under the weight of successive stresses. It is time to take the journey to Self and finally address what is begging to be seen.

This time you will recognize something different. This time YOU will offer your true Self. For you are the giver. You are your own remedy. You will tend to your Self. You will come to your Self. You will become.

Are you sighing your life sigh in grateful expectation that something is finally going to happen for you? Are you feeling the relief that is inside the tears that have been waiting to fall? Is contemplating your deepest You, as wondrous as the first snow fall? If so, you are touching the hem of your silken garment. You are touching your Self, your uniqueness.

This chapter addresses the preparation that must take place and what you can expect as you remove your own thorns. There is much attached to this idea of healing, of going beyond these hurts to your Primary Essence. Once you experience the purity of First Life, you will never be the same. The experience of Self is the permanent window to a new life. This new awareness is like the sun's rays touching the Earth for the first time, the original rain falling and beginning the cycle. It is you laughing with the joy of life.

There is opening in this peeling back, and what this exposure potentially creates is both positive and negative. There is responsibility and obligations to Self and others. There are freedoms and rewards that many of us declare as our highest ideals. But the bottom line is, we must deal with our minds, behaviors, belief systems and emotions. We deal with all of the human potential that makes each of us uniquely human. Serious stuff. Prepare, now, to let go.

DIRECTION OF ENERGIES

Psychotherapist healers, like myself, are surgeons without scalpels. We remove psychological pathologies through energy forms. If our patients become cured in the psychotherapeutic process, then this energy movement (change) has been successful. Healers redirect energies from a negative flow to a positive flow. Come to see that you can redirect your own energy, for you are your own healer.

Patients come to treatment with a multitude of issues which need redirection. I propose to them that their problems are like a plate of spaghetti noodles and we need to remove one noodle at a time from the plate. I remind them that it took years for them to collect all these noodles and it will take some time to work through and remove them. Time is a healing factor. If you break an arm, no matter what you do to accelerate the healing process, the arm needs one critical factor for the healing to take place: time.

I caution my clients that healing is a process, rather than an event. I tell them that they probably won't wake up some morning with an overnight healing. It's like a thorn that enters, festers, and is slowly removed with the proper salves, compresses, and tools. However, it is not just a waiting game...it requires some action.

There are two elements to psychotherapeutic healing: time and hard work. As hard work has a painful element, so is healing painful. The thorn not only hurts as it punctures and enters the body, it also hurts when it exits the body.

Are you willing to allow the same factors to work in your own healing? Are you willing to put in the time and hard work? These are questions you need to answer in total honesty. In the nakedness of your limitations and laziness, you need to accept the pain that will be involved as you awaken your Self that has been asleep for so long.

Prepare for redirection.

*

OBLIGATION TO SELF

We have many obligations, but ultimately we are responsible to only two entities: our Self and our Creator. I believe our other obligations are quite obvious and specific to our individual circumstance. Look into your life to see who or what begs for your attention and question each. Your first obligation is to Self to discover your own strengths and become free.

Fritz Perls, a great psychotherapist, said, "I am not in this Universe to fulfill other peoples' expectations of me. I am in this Universe to fulfill my expectations of myself. And if in that process they like it—fine. If not, fine too." How freeing! The bonus is you get to live your life. This is not as ridiculous as it may sound. Many people do not live their own lives. They are constantly living as they think they should, according to, or for someone else. In this process, they have denied themselves the opportunity to become strong. They have denied themselves, themselves.

The Native American way is to explore and define one's own value system. If you do not take the opportunity to explore yourself and to discover your meaning, what's the point? When in the eternal circle can this search be accommodated?

The Native American techniques that have been shared with me and that I now share with you, will direct you in this learning process. You will learn how to stop abusing yourself and become self-nurturing. Our spirit needs to become the bow that consistently shoots the four internal arrows of Recognition, Attention, Affection and

Approval. All people have an inherent need for these four valida-tions.

We all need to be recognized for the special person we are. We all need attention that nourishes our child within. We all need affection to heal our wounds. We all need approval for our life choices. These four needs can be met by Self. Once you learn to validate your own life choices, you will be free to experience and choose more of life. Self-validation is a powerful healing gift you will receive from this book.

To heal properly and to maintain psychological and spiritual health, we need to groom ourselves with these affirmations. We will then become a self-sufficient entity. Any recognition, attention, affec-tion, and approval we get from others will become a bonus, rather than a necessity for psychological survival.

Prepare to heal yourself.

MONKEY MIND

Many illnesses are of mental origin. Some Indians look at physi-cal disturbance as "mind creatures" that cause negative havoc. Many people mentally hold themselves hostage and repeatedly terrorize themselves with negative beliefs and thinking patterns.

Our thoughts are a reflection of our beliefs. If someone believes that women are inferior to males, their thoughts reflect that premise. And without a quantum leap, the domination of women can occur, as natural progression transforms beliefs into action.

For...
Beliefs beget values.
Values beget thoughts.
Thoughts beget emotional responses.
Emotional responses beget attitudes.
And attitudes beget behaviors and actions.

Therefore, if you want to redirect your actions and behaviors, ultimately you need to redirect your beliefs. As the lake reflects the shoreline, your thoughts reflect your beliefs. You need to conclude that you're a good person, good enough to feel adequate, competent and sufficient. You need to conclude that you are lovable and loved, that you belong. Realize that you are connected to the Universe.

Once you have confirmed your worth, you can experience psychological and spiritual support. You will no longer be held hostage by your need for validation from other people. Until then, this need is your keeper.

On this continuum of beliefs to actions, much needs to happen. The process takes precedent over the result. Time is required, action is needed. Experiencing life vibrations, reconnecting to Earth Mother, will enable you to return to your Self, to your basic beliefs. From there—your center—all things can change. Connecting to Great Spirit is the avenue for change to occur. You need to shift to your power source, from your head to your heart. You need to acknowledge that this power source exists in your own silence to effect change within you.

Learn to listen.

Listen to learn.

Deal with your monkey mind wandering wherever it wishes. Steer your mind and take command of your inner thoughts. Discipline your monkey mind by focusing on some thing or a thought, and when your mind wanders, bring it back to the task over and over again. In this process of conditioning, you will learn to focus and keep your soft eye on the tasks which shape your actions and behaviors. You will learn how to turn the lights on and off in your head. You will have your own mental rheostat. You will be in charge of your thoughts rather than your thoughts governing you. Proaction, rather than reaction. *So when your mind wanders, bring it back to the task with your intent.* Discipline is the arrow of deliberate direction.

Prepare for disciplined change.

FREEDOM AND REWARDS

The Native American teachings lead us to inner freedom and rewards. Our whole life becomes a series of lessons, insights and understandings that lead us down the path of enlightenment and wisdom. "A great learning must occur," says the Medicine Man, as he holds high this truth.

To come to know the world is to be wise.
To come to know oneself is to be enlightened.
To come to know the Universe is to be one with all.

To become free is to let go of the snake's tail and be present with yourself in the eternal now. Be in the world, but not of the world. The reward of that is satisfaction. For where there is no expectation, there is joy.

This joy can be yours.

For life to be a full, rich experience we must give as well as take. Serve as well as lead. Without the student, there is no teacher. Without the listening, there is no message. In Indian when we take from nature we also give something in return. Life is a continuous exchange of give and take to complete the moving circle. An Indian's wealth is measured by what he gives away rather than by what he possesses. This is the true meaning of Indian Giver.

When you are invited to an Indian birthday party, the birthday person gives all of his guests a present to honor them for being present. Not the other way around as in the non-Indian world birthday party where the guests bring the presents. Prepare yourself to give. Now is the time for giving. That will be your reward.

Hear the lesson of an old Indian story:

A foal was born to a great warrior's mare in the Spring. The warrior saw this as good, for his horse was slowing and he would soon need another. The

dapple gray colt promised to become a great
stallion, for his stature was like his father's. Yet
first, he became a colt of great mischief.

The warrior would spend many Summer days
chasing the colt, whose energy was not directed.
The warrior missed many meals tending after this
colt. He woke up many nights to check on the colt.

By Fall, the colt was ready to be weaned and the
warrior decided to tie him to a stake to keep him
from frolicking off. The young colt bucked, kicked,
pulled, tugged and tried in vain to uproot the stake
and free himself. As the leaves turned colors and
fell, the young warrior went each day to the colt
and exercised him. Each day the young horse
would be retied to the stake and fight to free
himself.

Winter came and Earth Mother claimed the stake
and held it tight as She became hard. By the first
deep snow fall, the colt's spirit weakened and he
accepted his rope.

The warrior was relieved. The colt finally quieted
and matched the silence of White Winter. Within
his wigwam, the warrior planned for Spring and
knew that he would soon need to have a stronger
rope and a larger stake.

Still, during the cold and the snow, the warrior ran
the colt. As Earth Mother softened to Spring, the
colt grew stronger. Soon, he was a beautiful and
powerful horse. As the peepers peeped, the warrior

looked for signs that his horse would pull the stake
up. But even as Ice melted into Earth Mother the
becoming stallion still accepted the length of his
rope and the strength of the stake.

For now the stallion's memory was the rope. His
sense of powerlessness was his stake. Although the
stallion grew even stronger in the years to come,
and could have easily uprooted it all, he never
tried, so he never did.

We, too, hold ourselves hostage by telling ourselves, "We can't,
when we Can!" Now is the time to say, "Yes!"

What's the worst thing that will happen if we become balanced,
centered and achieve higher states of consciousness? Will we become
too happy? Will we become too healthy? Will we sleep too well? Will
we become too enlightened? Too wise?

Don't worry about it.

Don't allow negative energy to interrupt your positive growth,
focus, and progression. Some of the greatest rewards of life are to
develop facial smiles and laugh lines, sleep well, become one with
nature, be able to sit still, do nothing, and fully enjoy the experience
of being alive. Coming alive—to be alive.

Don't miss the colors and the dance of the sunrise. Can the sunrise be too beautiful?

Prepare for your internal sunrise. It is time.

What follows are specific traditions that will teach you to come
to your self, experientially. Paths that will lead you to sunsets that
can not be too beautiful. Techniques that will help you peel back the
layers that hide your true Self. Traditions that will help you become.

So right now, turn off the lights in your head that illuminate your
thoughts and quiet your monkey mind. Now is the time to experience
your internal Self.

Listen.

Listen.

Listen to the Great Silence within.

For it is within this Great Silence that all good comes forth. Put your head on your pillow and hear your blood flow through your veins. Listen to your heartbeat. Listen to the drum, your Drum.

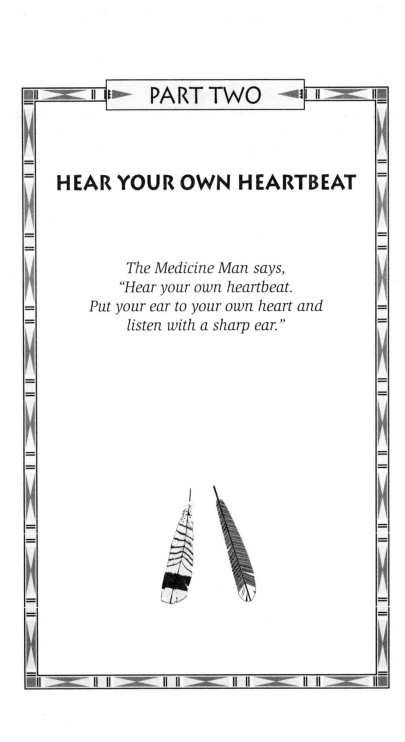

PART TWO

HEAR YOUR OWN HEARTBEAT

The Medicine Man says,
"Hear your own heartbeat.
Put your ear to your own heart and
listen with a sharp ear."

MISHOMIS

You found me among many.
You reach for my ache.
You teach me of healing.
My wounds you take.

Welcome. You have positioned yourself to be open to the ideas and the beliefs of "Old Age" wisdom. Rather than lecturing, these ideas show you ways to come to yourself. They will require you to experience. Through your experience, you will be able to comfortably address the uncomfortable. You will be able to befriend yourself, the most natural thing to do. You may look back on your past life with disbelief, and wonder, "How was it that for so many years I could not hear the messages that were being sent to me each day through the beating of my own heart? How could I not see the things that were in front of me each morning? Or feel the wonder that touched me each night?" You will feel different. You will experience life differently. You will want these differences to continue. You will crave more of the path. You will connect with the invisible.

How many of you are comfortable getting a body massage? How many of you have allowed yourself to feel the soothing touch of another human being? There are many people who have never experienced the joy of that feeling. How sad. I would guess that some of you have accepted this feeling, up to a certain point. A back massage, perhaps shoulders, or maybe even your feet. But have you ever experienced the relief given when your knees, fingers, toes, forehead, cheeks, ears, eye lids, nose, buttocks, underarms, and wrists are massaged? Have you ever given yourself permission to allow another human being to soothe you in this way? For many, this might seem frightening. To others the idea of total body massage might seem intriguing, that even your eye lids could feel this wonderful sensation. When you experience the feeling, "Please don't stop, just five more minutes," you have given yourself permission to receive the gift of healing.

Those who have never quite let go of their self-consciousness, cannot follow the healing touch as fully as possible. The message of the other person's fingertips never gets through. They have not learned to open up to the possibilities. They have not allowed themselves to receive this gift of healing and just let go.

I ask you now, to give yourself permission to follow the fingertips of the Spirit World, as they massage your entire being. All of you, not just the back of your spirit. Allow the following techniques to relieve your most sensitive areas, your most vulnerable recesses, the most hidden you. Like a newborn, trust in your most basic responses. Allow the child-like qualities to explore the messages the Spirit World gifts you. Do not get preoccupied with the fingers, but look to where the fingers point. Feel what the fingers touch.

It is time to massage your spirit. To hear your own heartbeat.

MISHOMIS

To massage your softness, we start with the hardest: The Mishomis[1].

---

[1] Pronounced: mi-SHOO-mis. Mishomis is the Ojibway word for Grandfather.

The invisible spirit energy of Mishomis is visible as the rock beneath our feet, the stones you throw into the lake, the mountains you view from afar. In the Ojibway language, Mishomis means Grandfather and is the collective male spirit energy which has amassed for thousands of years. Earth Mother, who is feminine, gives birth to rocks which in Indian are masculine (since their shell is hard and not of soft feminine substance). Through volcanic eruptions, and the tremendous changes it has undergone, Mishomis is the energy that has remained.

It is this energy and consciousness, from generation to generation, which has ridden the glaciers, seen the dinosaurs and the saber tooth tigers, and has contained the campfires of many Indian villages.

Mishomis has seen all, heard all, and understands all. Mishomis has experienced all, and therefore can understand all experience. The spirit of Mishomis knows your heart, your fears, your pain, and will help you find yourself. Wearing elegant robes of granite and gold, Grandfather's gentleness will serve you.

Mishomis contains the voice of the Ojibway people of the Old Migrations. The old spirits encased in their rock shell are ready to aid us on our path through this physical dimension. They are here to help us walk our path, just as we will be expected in the Spirit World to help those who walk their path in times to come. Grandfather Stone helps us to remove repressed and imprinted memories, emotional trauma, and the daily stressors of life.

As I write these words the first snowfall of the season descends, covering Earth Mother with a white robe for her winter rest. Can you recall a time when you fell on the ice and injured yourself? Take your finger and touch the body part that was affected. Hold that pose and imagine that as you walk outside, the sidewalk is sheer ice. How will this identified body part respond? The former injury will probably send a clear message to alert you to proceed with extreme caution. Our bodies communicate with our mind, spirit, and emotions. It is time to allow this obvious connection to connect with the Spirit World.

To do this you must first meet your Grandfather Stone. You will know your Grandfather when you see him. You may walk a stony beach for miles only to spot him intuitively, among the multitude. You will know, just because you will know. Both your spirit and Grandfather Stone's spirit will merge. As you find him, he finds you. A blind person who wants a seeing-eye dog may have experienced this truth. They don't pick the dog, the dog picks them from a room full of candidates. Once you embark on the search for your Grandfather-Mishomis-Stone you'll understand this communication level, for Grandfather will find you.

Go out now and allow your Grandfather to find you, for he will become your eyes to the Spirit World. When you return, hold him in your hand. Listen to the words that will open you to the experience of Mishomis healing.

GIFTS OF MISHOMIS

A rock has a state of consciousness and is programmed to break down and form soil in order to accommodate rebirth and nurturance. Have you ever driven through the Rocky Mountains and seen giant pine trees growing out of great solid rock formations? It seems impossible that anything could grow from solid rock, yet the rock shapeshifts[2] from hard-masculine to soft-feminine. From Mishomis to Nokomis[3]. From Grandfather to Grandmother. One within each other, to again repeat the cycle of birth. The pine cone, which is also programmed to repeat its life cycle in endless procreation, is accommodated.

The rock you have chosen is the vehicle for the energy you need to give and receive. Just as heat energy is transferred more easily through certain types of matter, so too, your spirit energy chooses

---

[2] Shapeshifts is a term to describe the transformation of state of existence.

[3] Nokomis is the Ojibway word for Grandmother. Pronounced: no-KO-mis.

Mishomis as nature's conduit. Grandfather's knowledge is unparalleled since the beginning of time.

See the kinship your Mishomis has with the Spirit World. It is time to appreciate their inherent connection and plug into the oneness of their Source. Allow Grandfather Rock to become your visible channel to the invisible Spirit World.

Earth Mother who is the source of our nurturance, comes from the Source of Everything. She takes the composition of former generations, grandparents, animals, trees, and all that has existed, and compresses their remains into Grandfather Rock. The stone then waits in patient stillness to help us walk the path of life.

Once you have selected a stone, cradle it in the palm of your hand and feel Grandfather's energy. The energy emitted is incredibly vibrant and consoling. You need to experience this energy.

This power is especially notable where great rock formations exist. Years ago, I was driving through the Rocky Mountains and stopped at a wayside. I stepped out. My feet grounded themselves on a massive layer of granite and absorbed the vibrant energy waves. The enormity of the majestic rock profile before me was overwhelming. In my awe struck state of consciousness, I saw the Majesty, I felt the power. I recall saying, "Gitchi Manidoo's[4] power is unlimited."

At that moment, the curtains were pulled back and these mountains of limitless mass revealed themselves as the creator's hand in apparent rest. I pondered the possibility that if the Great Spirit chose to flex His fingers, a cataclysmic consequence would result. This finger flexing is part of the endless topographical shifting that takes place over millions of years. Grandfather Rock is always, patiently, slowly, in silent motion to keep the sacred hoop fluid.

Have you experienced the energy yet? Do you recognize the power? When you can say yes, then it is time to begin.

With Grandfather Stone in your hand, feel the hardness. Connect with the energy. Befriend him. Take time to get to know him, so that

---

[4] Gitchi-Manidoo means Great Spirit in the Ojibway language. Pronounced: GI-chi MON-ee-doo.

if he was nestled among millions of other rocks, you could find his essence easily. Know him on a personal, intimate level. Acquaint yourself with his contour, his smoothness, his roughness, his lines and recesses, so even if blind, you could distinguish him from all others. With your eyes closed, feel his intent. Feel his openness, his readiness, his willingness to heal you. You are holding your healer in the palm of your hand.

Now think of the snake's tail that you have been trying to let go of, but continually return to. What emotions overwhelm you? What clutches at your throat? What memory tightens your shoulder, your neck, your jaw? What is your secret? It is the one that causes your heart to beat faster. Listen to your heart.

Whatever it is, whomever it involves, whenever it began, however it continues, look at it now and allow yourself to feel the energy it demands. The prayer to follow is the prayer of hundreds of years. Please follow it carefully, thoroughly, and with sincere intention. For only then will you experience the healing Grandfather offers you. Stop right now and allow time to relive its birth.

I invite you to say these words. Say them with your heart. Let your heart speak:

> Grandfather, you are strong for me. I feel your
> support in my hand. I feel your edges and your
> curves. I see your face that has seen thousands of
> years of living. Thank you Grandfather for waiting
> just for me.

> Thank you, Grandfather, for all you are about to do
> for me. Please wait for me just a little more. I need
> to be ready for your gift.

> I must hold onto my pain one last time. I need to
> experience the hurt, the agony, the ache. It has
> power over me. It controls me. Please wait for me
> Grandfather, as I let it control me.

I remember it all. I can see where my pain began. I
can smell what was around me. I can feel it in
total. Wait for me, as my heart's muscles push and
make my blood rush. Wait for me, Grandfather, for
my heart must ache. Wait for me as my heart cries.
It must cry. I must cry. The pain must wash me
before I can let go.

I hold all the pain in my heart, Grandfather. I am
ready to let it go. I am ready to give my pain to
you. Into your patient depth, I pour all of my pain.
With my soft eye, I follow it as it rushes to your
waiting arms. I say good-bye to the pain. I give it
all to you.

Thank you for taking my pain from me. Thank
you, Grandfather, for your gift of acceptance.
Thank you for wanting to heal me.

Now go to a stream, a lake, a brook, a waterfall, a water faucet,
or any water source and request the aid of the Water Spirits. Hold
your Grandfather Stone with respect:

Water Spirits, here is Mishomis. He waited for me
for many years. He has taken my pain and holds it
with his strength. Please, Water Spirits, cleanse
Mishomis of my pain. Relieve him of my negative
energy. Wash over him and free the pain. Fulfill
your destiny of cleansing the Universe and wash
Mishomis. Thank you, Water Spirits for your
assistance. Thank you, Water Spirits for your
healing.

Now, go and meet Grandmother Moon and hold your Mishomis up to her moonlight:

> Nee-ba-gee'-sis[5], see Mishomis. Mishomis has
> waited many years to accept my pain. He accepted
> my pain, and has now been cleansed by the Water
> Spirits. I ask you, Grandmother Moon, to permeate
> Mishomis with Sahgeen, your love and respect. Fill
> Mishomis with your gifts. Soothe Mishomis. Care
> for Mishomis. Fill Mishomis with love.

Now, cradle Mishomis in your hands and offer these words from your heart:

> Grandfather Stone, please gift me with your gifts of
> Moon tenderness. Share with me the positive
> energy you have received. I have yearned for love
> and respect. Thank you, Grandfather for giving me
> love. Thank you for giving me respect. My empti-
> ness where the pain once was, is now filling with
> your gifts. My heart now rushes with the tide of
> belonging. My broken Self is made whole. Thank
> you, Grandfather Stone for your healing. Thank
> you for your love.

Take all the anger inside of you and give it to Grandfather. Give it to him now.

Now put your sadness in your stone. Your Grandfather wants it. Your Grandfather is open to it. He can hold it. Give it to Grandfather. Your Grandfather traveled thousands of miles and millions of years to be with you.

---

5 Pronounced, NEE-ba-GEE-sis. Means, "the moon," which is Grandmother. Gee'-sis, pronounced GEE-sis, is "the Sun," which is Grandfather.

Take all your fear and give it Grandfather. Grandpa wants it. He can take all your fear and then some.

Now take all your shame, all the shameful messages from others and Self and put that, give that, to Grandpa. Give it to Grandfather.

Now take all your guilt. It is a biting feeling. Give your Mishomis your guilt.

Give Grandpa your frustrations. All your frustrations, confusion, and negatives need to come out. Get all this pain out. Get all of it out of you. Now.

Then wash Grandfather. Wash all of it out. The Water Spirits[6] want to wash it clean. They need to wash it out. Know the Water Spirits await to change you. Then fill up with Grandmother Moon. Accept the love that fills your Mishomis and become whole. Connect to the Life Source and feel peace.

Once you have experienced this emptying and filling, you can repeat this process whenever needed. Grandfather sits in passive readiness to console you and heal you, as he has awaited millions of years for you to ask.

---

[6] The Water Spirits are the most powerful of all. They teach us the mystery of the Creator. Know that something very soft transforms something very hard. They cut rivers through mountains, sculpt the Grand Canyon, rearrange entire landscapes.

AIN-DAH-ING AND MASH-KA-WISEN

Go inside, for that is where your home is.

You have activated the channel to the Spirit World by acknowledging and releasing your pain. Your willingness to allow the visible of this Earth, Grandfather Rock, to accept your pain and heal you, reveals your connection with the Spirit World. Have you let go of the snake's tail that preoccupies you with yourself? Have you given yourself time to experience the healing? Have you worked hard to revisit their power over you?

Have you thanked your Mishomis for becoming part of your new Self? Experience the act of thanking, for inside the thanking there are even greater gifts of joy and freedom.

How do you feel? Take some time to reflect on your new state of awareness. Become accustomed to taking your own emotional pulse. Try to identify, exactly, your condition. Hear your heartbeat anew and listen to how steady it is. When you peel back the painful memories of emotional trauma, the constriction on your heart loosens. The chains that have been demanding your attention fall away and your Primary Essence is revealed.

There is likely more to strip away, but you are now on the path that gravitates towards your authentic Self. Through the exercises to come, other painful memories that have been hidden up to now may surface to your awareness. If they do, you can repeat the previous Mishomis exercise, and further free yourself. I applaud your decision to address the pain, to feel its power. What I am asking you to do is not a simple task. It is demanding. Indeed, it is painful. Your courage to walk through your fear will be rewarded in ways you can not comprehend right now. The thorn begs for removal; realize your role as a healer and give this gift to your Self.

This is hard work. And it does take time.

But it doesn't take long to benefit from the gifts you are receiving, as you take the steps needed to heal yourself. You are your best healer. What your heart speaks as it beats within you, is only to be heard and known by you and your Creator. This bears repeating. *Only you and the Life Source will ever know you at this level.* The most intimate of all relationships is between you and your heart. Listen to your heart and continue on your journey.

AIN-DAH-ING

It is time to go home. The home within your heart is where your Primary Essence awaits. Ain-dah-ing[1] is this home. Ain-dah-ing is a sanctuary of peace and contentment. Here, you are safe from all of the worries and cares of the day. Ain-dah-ing is connected to your natural realm, yet is not affected by it. This is your eternal home, beyond time and space.

Some years ago, I became quite ill. I remember writhing in abdominal pain for two days. During those moments of terrible agony, I fought waves of pain that washed over me. Each movement I made intensified its hold over me. I was preoccupied with the relief that I could not find. Out of pure exhaustion, I finally gave up, surrendered to it, and became still. I began to follow my breath. Slowly and with

---

[1] Ain-dah-ing is our home within our heart. It is pronounced: AH-da-ning.

soft focus I followed my breath. When I was tempted to think of my pain, to give in to its demands, I simply brought my mind back to the task and continued to follow my breath. My body quieted. My mind went beyond thought. My emotions were still.

Inside the silence, I discovered Ain-dah-ing. I found peace. The revelation of this home inside has greatly affected my life. For this is the place of peace. This is where even death can not touch. This is the place where we begin and end, only to begin again. This is Ain-dah-ing. This is the experience of the Great Mystery.

To reach Ain-dah-ing we need to shift our awareness. We need to follow our breath. This, like all life cycle experiences, is a step-by-step process. Every step is important and necessary in order to connect to the power source which exists to change us. Each step in that direction is progress and needs to be valued and given respect.

To come home to Self, to become, to be, is a journey. Each step is necessary. Each step is priceless. Each step is worthy of your respect and honor. Do not be in a hurry to "get there." For there is no "there'. Indeed, there are only "here's." Stay with the now. Cherish the experience and concentrate on the wonder of each moment. This is not a contest, this is a journey into a beautiful landscape. If you look only for the sunset, you may miss the sunrise and the warmth of the day sun. You may miss the most beautiful and meaningful scenery to you. Your journey to Ain-dah-ing is as important as Ain-dah-ing itself. Pay attention. Experience. Each Now along the way awaits with a gift.

In the circle of this experience, ride the current of change. Be change.

The following exercise will guide you to your Ain-dah-ing. Here, you will experience change. In order for you to experience this healing technique, you will need thirty minutes.

Is there someone willing to aid you with a gift of healing? Have you thanked him or her for participating in your life journey? If so, instruct them to read each paragraph to you very slowly, and give you time in between, in the spaces, so you can experience each segment in total. If you do not know anyone to help you here, you can read these words into a tape recorder and then play it back to yourself[2]. You may choose to read to relaxing music or a drum beat. Allow these words to enter the sunlight of your own journey. Now begin:

This exercise will direct your mind to sweep your body clear of any stress and tension and will enhance your ability to relax and focus on the present rather than to wander off to the past or into the future. This exercise will take you to the calm part of your being, where your mind, body, spirit, and emotions interconnect. This exercise will take you to Ain-dah-ing:

Assume a relaxed position. I suggest you sit in a comfortable place.

Place your thumbs and middle fingers together in a circular connection.

Place the tip of your tongue on the roof of your mouth, on the tiny pallet, just behind your two front teeth, and follow your breath to your home that lives in your heart, Ain-dah-ing.

Find that part of your mind, which is called the mind's eye, just above your nose and between your eye brows. That is the part of your mind which watches everything that goes on within your mind, within your body, within your spirit, and within your emotions.

Close your eyes and watch your breath enter the tip of your nostrils. Experience that sensation. If your mind wanders, bring it back to the task.

---

2 For an audio tape of this exercise call (800) 983-0600.

Watch your breath enter the tip of your nostrils, and go into your nostrils. Experience that sensation.

Watch your breath enter the tip of your nostrils, go through your nostrils, and down your wind pipe. Experience that sensation and if your mind wanders, bring it gently back to the task.

Watch your breath enter the tip of your nostrils, go through your nostrils, down your wind pipe and into your lungs. Experience that sensation.

Watch your breath enter the tip of your nostrils, go through your nostrils, down your wind pipe, through your lungs and into your stomach. And if your mind wanders, gently bring it back.

Follow your breath to the lowest region of your abdominal area, deep down into your power center. Watch your breath enter the tip of your nostrils, go through your nostrils, down your wind pipe, through your lungs, through your stomach, to the lowest region of your abdominal area. Experience that sensation, and if your mind wanders bring it back to the task.

Watch your breath make entire cycles through your body. Watch your breath enter the tip of your nostrils, go through your nostrils, down your wind pipe, through your lungs, through your stomach, to the lowest region of your abdominal area. Watch where it reverses course, comes back up, through your stomach, through your lungs, back up your wind pipe, through your nostrils, and exits at the tip of your nostrils.

Watch your breath make entire cycles through your body. Experience that sensation, and if your mind wanders, bring it back to the task.

Become aware when you inhale, the air is cool as it enters the tip of your nostrils. Experience that sensation. Inhale—cool.

Become aware that as you exhale, your breath is warm as it exits the tip of your nostrils. Experience this sensation. Inhale—cool. Exhale—warm.

Become aware that as you inhale, your body raises, and as you exhale, your body lowers. Your body goes up and down.

And up and down...

Somewhat like a wave on the ocean, that goes up and down. And up and down. Remain aware of the raising and lowering of your body as you inhale and exhale, somewhat like a wave on the ocean, that goes up and down. And up and down.

Allow the skin on your forehead and your scalp to become loose, limp, and relaxed. The skin on your forehead becomes so smooth that the band of stress on your forehead slips off and falls away.

Your eyes become heavy—very heavy—and rest gently in their sockets.

Your tongue becomes thick and heavy, and rests gently on the floor of your mouth, while still allowing the tip of your tongue to rest gently on the pallet just behind your two front teeth.

Your jaw becomes very, very heavy. So heavy, that it takes the pressure, the stress, and tension off your jaw hinges, just below your ears. Your jaw is very, very heavy.

Your neck muscles are loose, relaxed.

Your shoulder muscles become so relaxed, you can feel the warmth and comfort settle in.

Your upper arm muscles are limp. Your elbows become loose and very, very heavy. Allow all the weight from your head, neck, shoulders and upper arms to rest gently in your elbows.

Your lower arm muscles are relaxed. Your wrists are loose. Your hand muscles become so relaxed that they feel warm and tingly. Your fingers become as light as cat whiskers.

Visualize tiny openings, approximately the size of dimes, in the center of the palms of your hands and allow all the stress and tension from your head, your neck, shoulders, arms, and hands to pour out of those tiny openings like water. All the stress and tension from your upper body are pouring out of those tiny openings in the center of the palms of your hands, like water.

Remain aware of the raising and the lowering of your body as you inhale and exhale, like a wave on the ocean, that goes up and down. And up and down.

Allow your back muscles to relax and the skin on your back to become very, very smooth.

Your chest muscles are limp, relaxed. The skin on your chest becomes so smooth that the band of stress around your chest slips off and falls away.

Your stomach muscles are loose, relaxed. Your abdominal organs are limp, relaxed. Your buttocks becomes so relaxed, you can feel the warmth, the comfort settle in. Your upper leg muscles are relaxed and become very, very, heavy.

Your knees are loose. Your lower leg muscles become so relaxed, they feel like wood. Your ankles are loose. Your foot muscles are so relaxed, they feel warm and tingly. Your toes become as light as cat whiskers. Visualize tiny openings approximately the size of dimes, in the center of the soles of your feet. Allow all the stress and tension from your back, chest, stomach, abdominal area, buttocks, legs and feet to pour out of those tiny openings like water. All the stress and tension from your entire body are pouring out of those tiny openings in the center of the palms of your hands and the center of the soles of your feet, like water.

Empty your body of all the stress and tension.

With your mind's eye, search your body for any remaining tension in any part of your body. If you find any stress and tension remaining, inhale and see with your mind's eye the part of your body that still has stress and tension in it. Grab hold of the stress and tension with your inhale breath, and sweep it clean of your body with your exhale.

Grab hold of the stress and tension with your inhale breath and sweep it clean and out with your exhale breath.

Your body is now void of all stress and tension.

Begin to inhale white light.

Inhale white light. Healing, white, light. Have white light penetrate every cell and part of your body. Continue to inhale white light so that it permeates your entire being. It surrounds your entire body, in a configuration of an eggshell, and encapsulates it in white light.

Continuing to inhale white light, shift your focus to your mind's eye, just above your nose, between your eyebrows. Have your mind's eye look up at the source of the white light. What do you see?

You have now arrived at the center of your being, where your mind, your emotions, your spirit and your body interconnect.

This is your eternal sanctuary within. How good it feels, how peaceful, how tranquil, how serene. Ain-dah-ing.

The answer is within yourself, and you are here.
You have arrived.

Within this place within, is where your spirit and
your Creator's Spirit connect. How peaceful, how
serene.

And know that you can come back to this place at
any time, because you now know the path within
to come here.

Enjoy this experience and continue to inhale white
light. White light.

White Light.

White Light.

When you are ready, I invite you to open your eyes.

And when you are *ready,* I invite you to open your eyes.

And when *you are ready*, I invite you to open your eyes.

GIFTS OF AIN-DAH-ING

How do you feel? Do you feel relaxed and calm? Do you feel
whole? Do you feel sufficient? Do you feel connected? Do you feel
full? The feeling you have now is what you've been looking for in
people, places, and things, but could never find. You were looking
outside yourself.

Now that you have come to Self, you can begin to *be* Self. You
have now completed another transition within your task of becom-

ing. You have learned how to center yourself. And how good it feels! There is an extra bonus for you at this juncture: You now know how to breath properly. Another gift from Gitchi Manidoo, to whom we say Migwetch.

Going to Ain-dah-ing is where you can tap the source of all blessings. This is how you can reach the source of greater balance. Here is where you are now able to tap your inner strengths. This happens, because you have quieted yourself enough to listen to your own heartbeat. To the great pulse of the Universe.

The gifts waiting for you are many. In the silent space between the beats, you discover intuitions. Here is where knowledge freely flows. Peace abides in the place of nothing. And insights occur while being quiet. Ain-dah-ing is the place where your heart rests, where your heart connects to the drum of life. Here is where you learn how to be capable and self-sufficient. In the home within your heart you will thrive.

MASH-KA-WISEN: A GIFT OF AIN-DAH-ING

Now that you have come to Ain-dah-ing, you have connected to the spiritual source of all. This force pours into a reservoir of Mash-ka-wisen[3], or inner strength. Mash-ka-wisen is one gift of reaching Ain-dah-ing and plugs you into the power of the Great Spirit. You can build your life with this inner strength. You will overcome many obstacles with Mash-ka-wisen.

This inner spiritual strength is accompanied by a sensation of peace, calm and tranquillity. You have tapped pure, positive, Creator energy. It is as if you have driven a pipe into the ground and the pure, unadulterated water surges forth to nourish and bathe you.

Mash-ka-wisen in the Anishinaabe[4] language means to be strong and accept help. The idea to stand like a rock (be strong and grounded) and move like a river (accept help and be fluid) conceptualizes this original definition well. It emphasizes the balance needed of oneself in order to be effective in this world. Remember the lesson of the willow? You must remain flexible.

On a spiritual level, Mash-ka-wisen includes inner strength. It is the bow of our spirit. This bow is capable of releasing incredible inner arrows of spiritual strength, which manifest themselves in positive thought substance, emotional fortitude, and physical perseverance. Mash-ka-wisen is an energy that emanates from Ain-dah-ing. Therefore, a connection is needed. Mash-ka-wisen is the process and progress in that shift. It is not a product. It is the experience, as you experience it, now.

Mash-ka-wisen takes you to your center so that you have a view of both sides. At your center, you have a window view of both the spirit and natural worlds. From this vantage point, you can now see things that before were not in your vision field. You will come to

---

[3] Pronounced: mash-KOW-sin

[4] Anishinaabe means those who were the ancestors of the tribes now known as Ottawa, Potawatomi and Ojibway.

intuitively understand things that were previously confounding. You have now experienced the opening to the "Light." You are the flower that bows and cups itself, to become a humble recipient of Grandfather Sun's illuminating rays. In contrast to your former closed spiritual position, you cannot help but respond as your spiritual petals unfold. This sacred flower is within you.

Mash-ka-wisen brings us to interconnectedness. It is at this inner-core level that our true nature can be the conductor, like a tree trunk, of God's pure love vibrations. How soothing. How satisfying. How fulfilling. Finally, our void is filled with the Great Spirit's nectar.

> Ah, Ain-dah-ing!
> Mash-ka-wisen is your gift to me.
> I look from your view and I can now see.
> I open up to your light and I can now accept help.
> I let you wash over me and I can now have peace.
> I let your energy move through me and I am now flexible.
> I fill up with your power and I am now without limits.
> I drink up your splendor and I am now strong.
> I come to your silence and I am now calm.
> Mash-ka-wisen is your gift to me.
> Ah, Ain-dah-ing!

FEAR

Mash-ka-wisen—inner strength—neutralizes life's fears. The Medicine Man says, "How can fear itself hurt you?" As you think about it, you will conclude that it can't. The only way it can hurt you is if you empower it and react to it by fight, flight, or freeze. If you allow it to paralyze you or cause you to fight or flee, it will then become your master. Where there is fear, there is a master.

Either you will master fear or fear will master you. But there will be a master.

We need to learn to respond to fear like the warrior does. When you approach, avoid, or arrest in reaction to fear, you have allowed instinctive behavior to dominate. We need to train our instinctive reactions. A warrior faces fear head on and is not distracted by it. The brave acknowledges fear's presence, but instead of reacting to it, clearly considers options and alternatives available and responds rather than reacts. Fear is then defused and neutralized and comes to no consequence. The warrior does not allow his emotions to cloud this thinking. It is like the rabbit who allows the sight of the wolf to paralyze him. His thinking is clouded because he believes he will go unnoticed by the wolf if he freezes in place. The rabbit pays the ultimate price as he allows fear to paralyze him.

Fear does not need to be an intimidator or master. Rather, fear can become a companion who alerts us to threatening situations.

My clients often think fear is external. External events may precipitate fear, but fear is an internal event. That may sound elementary, but we need to know where fear begins and ends or it is empowered by its own camouflage.

The warrior says, "If we don't face fear, we then walk with it." The warrior is alerted by fear, identifies its source, and responds by pro-acting, rather than reacting. When fear is isolated and removed from Self, then we are free to plug into our spiritual power resource. Otherwise fear will block this connection. Fear's vibration will be dominant, rather than the wonderful flooding vibrations of Mash-ka-wisen.

Every time you step through your fear, you become stronger and fear becomes weaker. The greatest fear is coming to know the Self. People are afraid to go within and explore themselves, but this is the ultimate journey.

Realize it's good to feel fear, but it's debilitating to engage it. Fear is like poison. It is good to know poison's potential, but it will not hurt you if you do not partake of it.

This is the story of a young brave who was in warrior training. Listen to hear of his Mash-ka-wisen. It is my turn to share this story with you now:

As a teenager, a young brave was tested to prove
that he was worthy of becoming a warrior. He was
instructed not to allow anyone or anything to
penetrate the village circle. So all night he was to
stand guard. As the night wore on, this young
brave struggled to remain awake, as he became
more and more tired. Just as he was about to fall
asleep, the brave heard a noise from the woods. He
looked up to see a powerful grizzly standing right
in front of him.

"Go away!" demanded the young warrior, although
he felt pure terror at the sight in front of him. "No
one can enter the village."

The Great Grizzly could not believe what he was
hearing. "Do you know who you're talking to? I'm
the fiercest animal of these woods. I can do
whatever I want to do, whenever I want to do it,
and no one or nothing can stop me!"

Although the young brave was terrorized and
could feel even his heart shaking, he announced,
"You cannot enter the village—even if it costs me
my life."

The grizzly was so taken with this young brave's
courage, that the bear decided to pull out his eye
tooth and one of his claws.

"Because of your bravery, I offer these for you to
wear around your neck. They are symbols of your
Mash-ka-wisen. They are for all to see," the great
grizzly proclaimed to the surprise of the young
brave. "But I give you an even greater gift," the

giant bear continued. "Because you have stood up
to your fear, you will no longer be frightened by it.
You have mastered fear by facing its terror. Therefore, when you hear your heart beat fast, be alert
to danger, but come to know that no fear will ever
rule you again."

Remember this story of the young brave and the grizzly. Listen to
your heart, follow your breath, and go within. Here you will find Ain-
dah-ing. Within its home, embrace the gifts you receive. Here, you
will find your own Mash-ka-wisen and fear will no longer be of consequence.

PART THREE

ALL BEAT AS ONE

Into the water's world she looked
To find where she belonged.
She found the answer staring back
It was her Self she found.

MITAKUYE-OYASIN

Your heard my cry in the darkest night
And answered with your tear.
I wonder where our tears all fall.
Is their cup the ocean here?

WE ARE ALL RELATED

Mitakuye-Oyasin[1] means we are all related. The connections to living, carry life. Mitakuye-Oyasin is the lifeblood of our existence. I cannot exist without you. I cannot exist without the Spirit World. I cannot be without the Great Pulse. We are all related. We are all connected.

Native American traditions honor these relationships between all people and things. Each time the stick strikes the drum head, we acknowledge the Great Connection between the physical world and the Spirit World. We honor the Web of Life. The drum speaks of these connections. The drum carries us back to Ain-dah-ing. The beat, the pulse, the essence delivers us back.

---

[1] Pronounced: mi-TAHK-wee-a-say

The interconnectedness of all of life vibrates through the heart-beat. The steady heartbeat tells us that everything is all right. The child in the womb hears his mother's drum keep a steady beat, the child takes consolation in the vibration. The old way was to bring the drum to the birth place. After the child was born the drum would sound steady, like a mother's heartbeat, to let the baby know that everything was as safe outside the womb as it was inside.

When Indians hear the drumbeat at Powwow, we come running. Earth Mother's heartbeat makes our blood rush, like her michi-zee-bee[2] (greatest river). The web of people who circle the drums feel this connection, and like strands, connect to the Great Pulse. We are taken back to the Silence, through the drum's rhythm. The beat that keeps us in our bodies connects us to Spirit World, as well. The drum is the great connector and divider. When your drum beats in the physical dimension you can connect to the Spirit World. When your drum stops beating, you cross the dividing line and return to Spirit World.

Listen to your heart's vibration, and you will connect to the natural world. Be present and listen to your pulse. Choose to walk along the pace of your own drum, and you will hear a story about yourself.

Listen to the space between the beats. The rest creates the beautiful rhythm, the silence sustains each beat. Like the strand that strings beautiful pearls together, the Great Pause connects all of life. Listen to the silence. It wants to tell you about your old spirit. The silence is the story we have forgotten. The story of where we came from. The story of where we go. The story of the web of life.

THE MIRROR OF MITAKUYE-OYASIN

All humans are the trusted keepers of the Divinity of the Great Spirit. If you take care of the image of the Spirit World made visible,

---

2 Pronounced: MICH-ee-ZEE-bee.

you take care of yourself. Honor your fellow travelers and see the divinity in all of them, the Yellow, the Red, the Black, the White, and the mixed. All life is sacred and humans need to acknowledge the image of the Creator in one another. Native American cultures have recognized for centuries that all living things have the reflection of *thou* in them. Discard the notion of superiority. We have elevated ourselves to the sacred *thou* position and have devalued the Sacred to the *it* position. We have put ourselves above and have crowned humanity as deity. We have taken the divinity out of the rock, the air, the animal and have reduced this divinity to *it*. Control issues and abuse have resulted. When we take the divinity out of the ordinary and put ourselves above, we deny our unity. We all share the same distance from the center of life. All our radiuses are of equal distance on the Great Circle. Do not fail to see that we are all one within each other.

Two summers ago the Mississippi River flooded. I heard a news reporter interview a civil engineer who said, "We cannot control the Mississippi River." The grandiosity of this statement continues to amaze me. Man over nature? Or God over Nature? Or Man with Nature? Which one is it? Until man respects the sacredness of all forms of life, things will disintegrate. Honor the Earth and we too, shall be honored.

Listen to our Elders who say, "When the bird dies, the song dies. Then man dies, for he has no song."

EARTH FAMILY

Mitakuye-Oyasin means we are all related. I am your brother. You are mine. We are part of Earth Family. Earth Mother loves her children, from the fish to the birds, from the blueberry to the oak, from the ant to the panther. We are all her children. We are all related. From her seas to her mountains, we are related. The weak and the strong, the rich and the poor, the young and the old, are all her children. We are all related. With love and hate, joy and pain, life and death, we are all related. Yesterday, today, and tomorrow. Here and there, we are all related.

Chief Seattle proclaims we are part of the Web of Life. What I do to you, I do to myself. What you give me, you give to the Universe. What the Universe gives, she gives to us. What I feel, you feel. What you become, I become. You are not alone nor am I. You are forever with me and I with you. We are brothers and sisters on the Web of Life.

A Navajo says, "What is, is," simply acknowledging all. We are related because we share the same breath. We are related because we are from the same place. We are related because we are. What is, is.

A Sioux Sun dancer says, "Ho-Hecatu-yelo." (That is the way it is.) Accept your relation, for that is the way it is. Embrace your relation, for that is the way it is. Hold hands with your relation, for that is the way it is. The Universe is one tree and we are her branches. Give shade to your brothers, support one another, and reach for the sunlight together. That is the way it is.

I share this idea of oneness that was once shared with me. I thank the Creator for the Web of Life I gladly participate in. Listen carefully to our relatives, as the drum speaks. Follow the drum to the many parts of the web and become the story. May your heart join the beating of my heart, as I offer these words to Gitchi Manidoo:

> All earth and sky things say Migwetch. From the
> bugs to each blade of grass, from the tree top birds
> to the fish in the sea, from you to me, we say
> Migwetch. From the low Earth to the great Sky, we
> hear the harmony of our Self, one another, Earth
> Mother, and Sky Father. We join in this song to
> become of one mind and one peace.

> We listen to the pulse of life and thank Earth
> Mother, for you are the life giver. We hold you in
> high regard, for we know you carry the secret of

creation in your womb. We are your flesh and roots. All from Earth returns to you. The spirits of our ancestors are held in your rocks, as we, too, will be welcomed back to your breast as clay. Our mother, you nurture us and provide everything we need. And your mountains reach to Sky Father. For this we say Migwetch.

Sky Father, we look to your blue blanket that covers us. Your clouds, thunderers and four winds provide for us. When our Grandfathers beat their drum, we hear your thunderers cross the sky. The drum wakes Earth Mother each spring and your warm winds grow things. Your winds change the seasons and move the breath to the Four Directions of East, South, West and North, to be again and again shared by all of our relatives. For this we say Migwetch.

We say Boo-zhoo[3] to our cousins—the Star People. In nighttime harmony, you sing your chorus to Grandmother Moon's song. Your torches guide us home. Your dancing warms our heart. For this we say Migwetch.

Grandmother Moon, from your nighttime perch, you watch over us when Grandfather Sun sleeps, and you reflect his dreams. You are the Grandmother of all life, of all nations, of all women. Your moon cycle is in harmony with women everywhere and the power of birth is again proclaimed. You teach us balance, for after day, there is night. You

---

[3] Boo-zhoo means hello.

caress the waters, causing the tides. You leave your sweet scent in the morning dew. We listen to your song with our soul's ear. For this we say Migwetch.

All creatures bow in thankful homage upon the first rays of light and warmth to you, Grandfather Sun. You give us light each day to complete our purpose. Your light supports growth and all needs are filled. Your strength is healing and comforting. Your rays reach to touch our beating hearts, and give us joy. For this we say Migwetch.

In the way of the sacred pipe, making the invisible —visible, and of happy heart, we say, Gitchi Migwetch[4] to Gitchi Manidoo for this sacred cycle. All is connected in this way.

INTERCONNECTEDNESS OF SEVEN DIRECTIONS

This Web of Life hears the echo of all things. Mitakuye-Oyasin asks you first to see, then to know, how all is one. May you understand that the doors to the East, South, West, and North, along with the In direction to Earth Mother and the Out direction to Sky Father, are there to support you, to teach you. Become the seventh direction,

---

[4] Big thank you.

so that you are one with the Sacred Hoop, complete the circle, and define your own purpose.

Moccasin Mike taught, "Respect all." He respected the fly that circled his head, and the horse that became his feet. He understood that the extinction of even the tiniest fly brings loneliness into the souls of all the directions, for the Family is saddened when it loses a relative. Many creatures have already disappeared and they are missed. We have fossils to remember some of our lost relatives and these pictures remind us to respect. Not a day passes that another creature family is forever lost. Earth Mother, Father Sky, Grandmother Moon, Grandfather Sun and the Four Directions—East (Wa-bun-noong'), South (Zha-wa-noong'), West (Ning-ga-be-us-noong') and North (Gi-way-din-noong'), cry for their lost children and grandchildren.

Abuse begets abuse, violence begets violence and respect begets respect. Which way are we going?

We need to listen to these words of Sitting Bull, "If a man loses something and goes back to carefully look for it, he will find it." We need to return to the old ways to find our lost treasures. We need to go back to Mitakuye-Oyasin and honor our relations with respect.

All is interconnected, has a transpersonal connection, and a mutuality of experience. If my ax strikes brother tree, what is my experience in that moment? What is brother tree's experience in that moment? What is the ax's experience in that moment? What is the forest's experience in that moment? What is the Universe's experience in that moment? What is the collective experience—of all—in that moment? The experience emanates and vibrates with repercussions.

From this interconnectedness, this relationship, comes the essence of purpose. The purpose of all things does not stand alone. The purpose of all things contributes to all relation. This interconnectedness becomes an endless series of life cycles. All things are in perpetual progression. Sacred and eternal, our purpose fulfills the greater purpose.

Birth, death, and rebirth.
Birth, death, and rebirth.
Birth, death, and rebirth.

When I was five years old, my grandfather took my hand and led me into the woods. We searched the forest floor until we found a fallen pine tree. Its death had occurred long before, and it was now blending into the soil beneath it, its bark long gone. With tenderness, my grandfather took my hands and helped me plant pine seedlings in the waiting arms of the log. The log welcomed the new seedlings and gave of itself, in order to give to its relation. Grandpa knew of birth, death, and rebirth.

From the pine tree example we can look within ourselves and experience the same sacred purpose. We need to put our ego, the "ME," to death in order to experience a rebirth to the "WE." Only then can we transcend and experience Oon-da'-di-zoo-win'[5]: our birth to another state of consciousness, connecting us to all.

Can you see we are one in each other? We are of the same essence. We are all born from Earth Mother and return to Earth Mother.

I love the lyrics, "It's a treat to beat your feet on the Mississippi mud." One of my favorite things to do is to stand in the mud and slide around barefooted. I am simply dancing on myself! We are made from mud and will revert to mud, for we are a fine mixture of Earth and Water. Next time you get mud on your carpet, don't panic. You're just looking in the mirror before your time! Experience yourself!

You are the connection between birth and death. You are the active link between the past hoop and the forthcoming hoop. This is your moment to experience. To live. To suffer. To enjoy. To transcend.

Get into the cadence of the Universe. Look up. Don't get stuck with what's on your limited level. Learn from the clouds. They are soft, but have strength. Watch the eagle as it ascends. Draw your attention to the Creator's realm. Your joy, right now, is when you find the awe, when you can hear the music of the Universe.

The next time you drive down the highway, turn on your favorite music and watch the birds dance to the vibration. Wonder what the

---

[5] Oon-da'-di-zoo-win means birth and is pronounced ON-da-DEE-zoe-win.

birds see as they soar between the peaks. See with Eagle's vision. Hear with Wolf's ears. Feel with Tree's branches. Touch with Caterpillar's feet. Smell with Bear's nose. Speak with silence.

Seize the moment. Catch it, grab it, embrace it. The purpose of your existence is to experience life. Feel it. Come alive. Live it. Feel the vibration. Vibrate, dance, sing, jump, skip, hop. Become a child again.

Live life as your hoop fades into ever-ness. You will have these moments to recall. Imprint the now!

I often visit the white pines that Grandfather and I planted. They are now over fifty years old and tower with majestic beauty. I remember their beginning. I remember the part I played, as my young hands touched the softness of their new needles. Today, I stand beneath their boughs in awe, and hear the song they sing. They whisper the song of Mitakuye-Oyasin. The old decaying log lives on in their branches. It is the song of birth, death and rebirth. It is the song of all, the song of cycles.

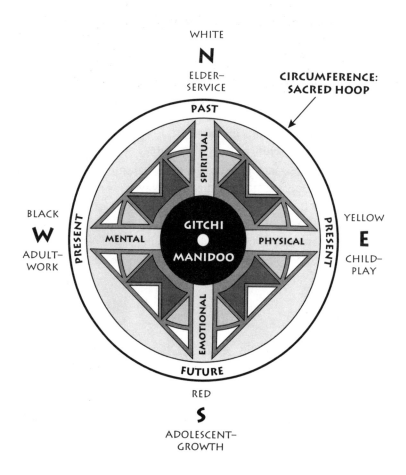

THE CIRCLE OF LIFE

THE CIRCLE OF LIFE

"Mine Moon!"
the little one shouted,
for she understood the Circle.

THE SACRED HOOP

One night before drifting to sleep, I had quieted my mind in order to connect with my Ain-dah-ing. The Great Spirit's voice was able to enter through passages that I had not consciously opened. In that place of awake but not awake, I was filled with complete understanding that the Great Spirit was circular. This sudden realization filled me with rare certainty, and in that moment, I consciously joined the Sacred Hoop.

We experience life cycles from the moment we are born: of day and night, from up to down and back up again, from in to out, life is circular. The seasons, the cycle of death and life, the moon, the stars, the planets, the pebbles that enter the lakes and create circles within circles, even the seven directions, show us that life is circular. We live on circles, we live beneath circles, we live in circles, for Earth Mother and Grandmother Moon, who give us our substance and watch over us, are also circular. The Great Circle is the Parental Guardian of all circles.

The Sacred Hoop encompasses the cycles of all things, and joins them together so that all energy is in balance. The Sacred Hoop represents the journey you take now. It symbolizes your connection to the invisible, as well as the visible.

To return to health, to return to life, you must return to the Circle. The Sacred Hoop is the Great Circle, the web of life. It circles the Source of all and is alive with universal vibrations. We follow its direction, we take this path to become. The Sacred Hoop represents the eternal configuration of the Creator. It contains a constant and consistent re-creation of itself.

Mitakuye-Oyasin reveals our connection to all of life. Now it is the time to see the separation of all of life. In the circle of life, all things come together, connect and then separate again, only to repeat this cycle over and over.

A circle is complete and never ending, yet to be a healthy traveler on the circle of life, separating of yourself is necessary. You do not separate from the Sacred Hoop. You separate only from temporary situations, from circumstances. When death comes full circle, you separate from your body, to live again. You separate from pain to fill up with joy, like the bear who separates from the fur that is not needed in Spring. See the separations you must make in order to enjoy the journey on the Sacred Hoop of Life.

The Sacred Hoop flows with the waters of change, emptying and filling. You are eternally connected to the Great Circle. All of life requires you to constantly separate and connect to new life choices and situations.

The dichotomy of personal separation and universal connection to the Hoop of Life is captured in my dream. See my Vision. Hear the Thunder. Touch Its Hoof. Both separation and connection are necessary aspects of the eternal circle.

Thunderhoof

Into the Silence, I heard your thunder.
Beyond the horizon, I felt your beat.
Entering my heart, I knew your Spirit.
Thunderhoof, you have come for me.

My eyes were clear with anxious searching.
My ears were keen to hear your breath.
My arrow flew to meet your softness.
My voice called out to meet your death.

You fell and my heart paused to meet you.
You looked at me, I felt your pain.
You left your family and gave your Spirit.
Your tears joined mine in the misting rain.

See your robes warm my children.
See your bones prepare my food.
See your flesh become my body.
See how all of me is you.

Let your Spirit roam where I roam.
Let you recognize my call.
Let you hear my invitations.
Let you experience the joy of all.

Into the Silence, I will join your thunder.
Beyond the horizon, I will feel your beat.
Entering my heart, I know your Spirit.
Thunderhoof, you have danced with me.

Do you see that in order for the buffalo to connect and contribute to the Sacred Hoop, separation was necessary? You must be willing to separate from attachments (both positive and negative) as you participate on the Circle of Life. The Great Circle is the strongest pillar of support there is. Build your life on it. Find your strength here.

The Sacred Hoop asks you to empty yourself of yourself. The buffalo gave up its life for all of life to receive. An Elder closes the flap on his lodge in order to open the door to Ain-dah-ing. The river empties so the buckets can fill.

The story of the Indian Council reveals the balancing and emptying needed in order for the Sacred Hoop to be engaged. The Council Circle understands separations. Hear how all heartbeats around the Council were touched by the listening of one:

The Circle of Mitakuye-Oyasin

The moment had come for the tribal members to decide whether to move on or to stay. All were present, from the honored women to the respected Elders. It was a glorious night, when the dance of the stars overhead would have few audience, for all brothers and sisters would sleep well. It was a night of warm wind spirits, of calm clouds. Grandmother Moon's full face looked down[1].

---

[1] Women who are on their moon cycle are not allowed to sit in any sacred ceremony. This is because the woman has within her the sacred power of birth and sacred ceremonies are a spiritual rebirth. The power of birth cannot clash with the power of rebirth. Indians respect this separation. Women are not discriminated against. On the contrary, they are held in high regard as they come full circle on their moon cycle.

The Medicine Man reached into his pouch and pulled out kinnikinnick, sweet grass, and cedar. Pinched between his fingers, he held it high for Grandmother Moon to see. With words of Migwetch, he let the medicine softly fall over the hot fire, and its essence joined the invisible with tiny sparkling lights that danced on the fire logs. And fireflies joined the dance with their twirls of silent paint.

Above the soft black headdresses of the men and women sitting around the fire, the sweet scent of smoke circled, blending the invisible with the visible. The connection to the Spirit World was made and the meeting could continue.

"Boo-zhoo" was heard from voices circling the fire as the invisible Spirits that had been invited to this important meeting now sat next to their brothers and sisters of the visible world.

The sound of every heart was important. The Chief would not speak until all were heard. The Elders would speak first.

"It is time to leave," the first one said. "The buffalo have not traveled this way for many moons and the berries have all dropped to Earth Mother. We must leave to find food."

"I disagree," spoke another. "There are plenty of fish in the river and we have stored the grains to fill our stomachs. We are settled here. And Grandfather Sun still warms the ground. Feel it. It is warm."

All listened intently. No one spoke until it was
time. All emptied their own thoughts, as they filled
up with the words of their brothers and sisters.

Finally, after her Elders had spoken, a young
woman looked up. "I have felt the cool breeze of
the North. I look in the waters and see less fish.
My stomach hungers for Brother Buffalo."

"I say we leave, now!" came the energy of another
young member.

But the Chief said nothing. He waited until all had
spoken. He waited until the old and the young
listened to each heart, until the hunters and the
mothers voiced their needs, until the weak and the
strong emptied their experience.

Only then did he speak. And only then of equal
voice. "Earth Mother has emptied herself for us
and for that we say Migwetch. Father Sky has
given us good days and for that we say Migwetch.
Grandmother Moon has blessed us with her beams
and for that we say Migwetch. Brothers and sisters,
you share a voice that is strong. Now is the time to
separate from this soil to find a new home. We
must continue to follow the Sacred Circle of life, to
where Father Sky, Mother Earth and Grandmother
Moon can again gift us. We can then gift them our
full life, our Bimadisiwin. Ah Ho."

The Indian Council Circle shows how all energies, all people, all
of life has its place reserved on the hoop. Looking at this truth and
living it are not the same. To really live it, you must engage the Sacred

Hoop and respect the life of all those on the hoop. Manifest Mitakuye-Oyasin. Relate, connect to your sisters and brothers. See the similarities, not the differences. Recognize that water is ice, as well as vapor. Hear the one heartbeat and embody the awe of life.

Our life experiences demand constant interaction. The process of living is a dynamic dance of yield and accept, which follows the ever-constant Sacred Hoop. As we accept our breath, we yield to its departure.

The Sacred Hoop silently speaks of ongoing life struggles. It speaks of agonies and fears, of the pain we must empty. The Sacred Hoop is about coming to center and knowing Self, letting its blanket of comfort surround you. When you have discovered the power of Ain-dah-ing, you understand Ain-dah-ing. You are allowed to be you. To be. To coexist in peace with all other members of the Web of Life.

Inside Ain-dah-ing, in your home within your heart, you are open, honest, clear, direct, and calm. These are the gifts of Ain-dah-ing.

This is the state of being in Ain-dah-ing. This is who you really are. The Sacred Hoop asks you to share these treasures with the world outside Ain-dah-ing. Share these gifts with those you meet on your journey, on the outside Hoop of Life.

Like the Council, listen with open ears.

Follow your path with honesty.

Fill your bucket with clear waters.

Speak with direct tongue.

Move with calm clouds.

This is the way of the Sacred Hoop. Practice these things as you travel on your journey to your Self.

Remember the feeling of opening yourself to the experience of Ain-dah-ing. It is comforting and filling. Like soaking in Grandfather's sunlight, it is the beginning to greater understanding. On your journey in this life, on the Sacred Hoop, work to become truly open. Allow others to see inside of you, just as you allow your Self to see out. Lower your defenses, trust your response to the now. You are present with what exists at this moment, both inside and outside of you. For even on the Hoop of Life, you can be here in Ain-dah-ing.

Open completely to honesty with your Self. Honesty follows the way of the hoop. It is given and accepted and then returned in full circle. Dare to see you as you are. Dare to show your true Self to those you meet. Accept the pain that honesty must bring, as well as the joy that flies on honesty's wings. For you are free. The flower, folded up at night, looks at itself, yet shows its beauty to all the world during the day. Be the flower of Ain-dah-ing.

Fill your bucket with clear water. Know your Self and your intentions. Give focus and purpose to your needs and desires. Give others the gift of understanding, for when you are deliberate and specific, you connect to other beating hearts with honesty and openness. Gift others the clear waters of Ain-dah-ing.

Speak with direct tongue. Face what you must. Do not run from fear, nor push through it. Commit to being open, honest, and clear with your brothers and sisters. Give yourself permission to express your heart, for Ain-dah-ing should not be kept a secret. Now is the time for your minds to meet, and your spirits to join. From your inner Self, share your Ain-dah-ing.

Calm waters originate from the depths of your Ain-dah-ing pool. Reveal this discovery through gentle strength. Allow your breath to bring in peace and tranquillity. Your calm Self will spread. Your calm is calming. Ain-dah-ing gifts flow easily when you are calm. Be the calm of Ain-dah-ing.

Be all of these things on the Sacred Hoop of Life.

The journey on the Sacred Hoop is seldom easy. As you apply the gifts of Ain-dah-ing, the emptying you must face (pain) is necessary and allows you to fill with other spiritual gifts. The pain has a purpose. As uncomfortable as it is, it is what you must work through in order to transcend. Without the mountain to climb, you cannot climb the mountain. Without the climb, there is no transcendence. Without the transcendence, there is no point in life.

Life is loss. We are constantly emptying our bucket through loss so that we can refill it again. This emptying is necessary, is desirable.

Have you acknowledged the necessity of both separation and connection? Reflect on times in your life when your bucket was empty.

Have you filled it with clear water? That is your privilege, that is your gift from the Spirit World. Reflect on times in your life when your bucket was full. Have you emptied it? That too, is your privilege, your gift to the Spirit World. Once you understand the dance, you can empty your container of pain and fill up with joy. It's your bucket, you know.

The stages of personal loss beg for your acceptance. Through acceptance you are free to move on the Sacred Hoop and implement Ain-dah-ing gifts of honesty, openness, clarity, directness and calmness. To accept one's problems, in the Indian way, is to accept the sun's rising and setting. It just is. It is part of life. Mountains are needed to climb. Accept.

Expect the sun to rise and set. Expect the mountain to appear. But only focus on the mountain when you meet it. Only climb it when you must. Only see it when it is there. Expect.

Climbing the mountain may make your legs ache. Spiritual waters can refresh you if you pause long enough to drink. Peace awaits to fill your loss. Have peace.

Gratitude is the greatest gift you can give or accept on the journey of the Sacred Hoop. It balances regret. Say Migwetch.

The Sacred Hoop concept is immense. It is about life cycles, about the journey of life, the emptying and filling, and about connections— Mitakuye-Oyasin. It embraces all forms of existence. The Sacred Hoop emphasizes circular thinking patterns, intuition, creativity, poetry, art, emotions, and appreciation of beauty. For life is circular.

In the silence of Ain-dah-ing, do you see your role on this circle of life? Be glad of your role, for you are the honored guest on the Sacred Hoop.

THE MEDICINE WHEEL

The Medicine Wheel is the Great Symbol for Life. It is considered to be the center and source of all things. From it all things flow. It becomes a reconstruction of life cycles, the symbol of rebirth and the origin of life. Never ending. Never beginning. To understand your Self, you need to quiet your mind to your own Ain-dah-ing, and open to the message of the Medicine Wheel.

The Medicine Wheel has three basic parts: 1) the circumference, 2) the directions, and 3) the center.

The Circumference is the Sacred Hoop. It represents the circle of life, the journey, the connections and separations needed, the life cycles that circle the Source of all. It reminds us of the gifts of Ain-dah-ing that we apply on our journey in life. The circumference moves into time, yet is connected to the timeless center.

The Four Directions represent the balancing we need in order to live fully. East, South, West, and North direct us to greater understanding of Self. We follow the arrows of the directions and come into balance.

The Four Directions organize all things. They bring us the life cycles and keep them renewed. The fabric of the Four Directions bring predictability and order. All cycles follow their form. Native American tradition calls on all directions in the course of life. The Medicine Wheel reminds us that we need to look to different ways in order to understand, to prepare for our listening experience.

The color to the **East** direction is Yellow. The first rays of morning sun bring the new light of innocence, like the white feather of the Eagle, to the darkness. It is the filling of the night container. It is a birth, an infant. It is the conception of a new day. It is the spring of the year stimulating new growth and burgeoning life forms. It is the explosion and creation of life from darkness. The is from the is not. The something from the nothing. This is East direction.

The color of the **South** direction is Red, the color of Earth Mother. South represents summer and adolescence. It is hormones exploding, experimentation, and invigorating growth spurts. The Self expands and grows outward as peer conformity begins to replace parental dominance within the socialization process. The separation from parents within the natural process begins. As the East grew upward, the South grows outward. It is a time for confusion which is the precedence of wisdom, the time to collect one's identity and the time of the vision quest. This is South direction.

The color of the **West** direction is Black. The sun trail takes us to this direction and into the cavern Self, where we come to see Self in the deep, dark, still waters within. The mirror of these bear-cave-waters, reflect our essence. This is the autumn of our life, the adult years. It is a time for knowledge and bundling it into the wisdom we have collected along our life. This is the time for us to throw off the shoulds and should-nots. They are no longer needed, for we have already become socialized by them. It is time to empty our bucket of these things (black), so that it can be filled again with wisdom (white). We need to empty the bucket so that it can be refilled with what we have come to value as individuals rather than what we have been handed by others. It is the time to live our own lives, rather than living someone else's. It is time for us to fill our emptied bucket, so that we become fulfilled. Fill your bucket with deep internal waters rather than the waters of the world. Be of Self, but not selfish or self serving. This is to become mature. This is West direction.

The color of the **North** direction is White, which is the accumulation of all colors. It is all consuming and solidifying. It is a time for enlightenment, a time to come to essence, to be purified and refined. It is a time to wear the white crown of Elder enlightenment. From this suspended state of consciousness flow the eternal waters of the spiritual river of life—the wellspring of the life cycle. From this spiritually dominant position will flow the spring waters of new vitality, for springtime rejuvenation. The North contains shifting spiritual ice sheets that move under great pressure. A new spiritual construct results. A Grand Canyon of Self emerges. The Northern Lights teach us how both light and darkness simultaneously emanate from the same essence, that they are complimentary, one in each other. These dancing lights endlessly empty and fill one another, enjoying one another's presence, and produce a glorious mystery of separation and connection. Darkness accents the light. From the North all will be renewed. This is North direction.

Beyond the Four Directions, we are asked to go down—to the fifth direction of **Earth Mother**. The color of the fifth direction is Green. This color reminds us that we need growth in our lives, and that Earth Mother nurtures our growth. Earth Mother is our connection to life.

The sixth direction is the color Blue. The direction is outward, to **Father Sky**. The sixth direction reminds us to monitor our lives, for it is in the sixth direction where the final evaluation of our life choices will take place. The sixth direction connects our present world with the world which we are moving toward.

The seventh direction is **You**. You are the seventh direction, both physically and spiritually. You are part of the hoop of life that intersects Eternity. This is the direction where you will recognize your role in life, become your Self, and will give of yourself.

When you see someone dancing in Powwow with small mirrors on their regalia, it is to reflect your image, validating this seventh direction. Therefore, I invite you to pick the color that best represents you, so the mirror of life may reflect your essence.

The Directions speak to the organizing power of the Sacred Hoop. We need to return to each direction to fill ourselves with their gifts, and to become the Seventh direction.

HEALING TECHNIQUES OF THE FOUR DIRECTIONS

The Four Directions of the Medicine Wheel help bring you into balance. They have been used by medicine people (healers) and individuals for healing. They remind us to look to each day and check our balance.

We can only touch other beating hearts when we are balanced and centered, for we become vulnerable like Brother Snake when we overextend. To be unbalanced is a very painful position. To be unbalanced means to feel tightness and fear. As we lean one way or another, we forfeit the muscles that beg to be in balance; not only physical muscles, but spiritual, psychological, and emotional muscles as well. A prolonged extension in any one direction builds rigidity, obsessions, and pain.

The application of the Four Directions will help you achieve balance. It encompasses all of the healing techniques so far given. You will be asked to apply the insights you have gained. Stretch your Self to find your balance and achieve a deeper healing.

It is time to come into balance. It is time to move with the fluidity, the graciousness of the eagle.

Listen to the directions sing the song of life's stages.

East

The spirit of the Eastern direction is the sunrise, the color yellow, and the new life of spring awakening from its deep winter sleep. Listen to the dandelion tell this story:

Dandelion Song

I dance in Spring Wind.
I connect to Earth.
I open to Sun.
I reach out for Sky.
I stand now as One.
I dance in Spring Wind.

All is here for me to grow.
I remember you before me.
I dream of soft flight.
I move with the day.
I sleep with the night.
All is here for me to grow.

I dance in Spring Wind.
I wonder where I end.
I wonder where I start.
I am circled with my scent.
I belong and I am part.
I dance in Spring Wind.

As young children we all danced with dandelion joy. We celebrated as we painted our faces with dandelion yellow. Our parents were our view of the world, our guidance, our validation. We were ducklings following our mother's tail, ready to offer our dandelion bouquets. When you are empty of joy, return to the East direction and fill up with the wonder of childhood.

South

As we grow into adolescence, we contain the spirit of the Southern direction—the color red, the color of Earth Mother's heart. It is the time of summer and exhilarating growth, experimentation, and knowledge. In this life position we look to our peers for validation and approval. Conformity is paramount. The need to belong is strong. This is a time of the socialization process, when friends know everything, and parents know nothing.[2] When you are emptied of understanding, return to the South direction for the energy to grow and change. Fill up with its gift.

---

2 Recently, I read a sign in a restaurant which stated, "Hire a teenager while they still know everything." How appropriate!

West

As we enter adulthood, we move to the spirit of the West direction, the color black, and the autumn of life. These are our harvest years and we enter the darkness of introspection. This is the time in life when we claim our own point of reference. We take what we have learned from our parents as children in the Eastern direction, keep what is productive for us and discard the rest. We sift through what we've learned from our peers in the Southern direction and we separate the helpful from the hurtful. We develop our own belief and value systems rather than echoing those of others. We become ourselves and come to our own conclusions rather than quacking like a duck in accolade of others. It is at this time that knowledge is converted to wisdom. When you become confused by life's distractions, return to the West direction and find the wisdom of adulthood.

North

As we approach the white door of the spirit of the North direction, we are held in high regard as grandparents. Our white hair is our headdress of snow purity. It is a time for rest and inner reflection, a time to touch the Creator's White Light. A time for enlightenment. You don't have to wait until you are seventy before you can achieve all this. You can do it now. When you learn how to empty Self, you can turn to the North direction and fill up with the Eternal. You can wear the headdress now, because the sacred hoop is eternal and knows you, not your age. There is no time in the Eternal, just the moment.

The Center of the Medicine Wheel is Gitchi Manidoo. The Great Spirit is eternal and does not move. It is the focal point, the axis, the essence of all life. The hub of the Medicine Wheel is the unending presence of the now. The Source of All is out of time. The Creator is eternal, limited by neither time nor space. The center is the timeless, eternal, God. The eye of the Medicine Wheel is as steady as the eye of the Thunderbird, the never-ending brightness of the Sun. The eye of

God reaches further than the sun's rays. It sees into the past, present, and future. It is the White Light that permeates our Ain-dah-ing. The eye of the Great Spirit holds timelessness; the memory of future and past blend with the present.

All is now. Now is all. Step into the eternal light and be present.

THE CENTER OF TIME

Native Americans wear the concept of time like a loose blanket, to be shed like the snake's skin, if necessary. Indians pay attention to the present, not the future of appointments, the ticking of clocks[3].

Learn the lesson from the hawk. Visualize Brother Hawk as he engages the poisonous snake—totally present, rhythmically merging with the snake's supple moves, and mirroring the death dance of snake. See the snake overextend himself with a strike. Like a bull fighter using his cape to blind the bull, watch as hawk uses his wing to blind the snake. This he does, as his talons simultaneously sink deeply to arrest the snake's strike. This precise movement in the present accomplishes the difficult task through a vigilant series of small acts. Inch by inch. Moment by moment. Learn from Hawk.

Learn from Eagle. This summer, I was fishing with my friends on the reservation. High in Father Sky we spotted Brother Eagle riding the currents. So high, he was barely visible. Soon he was traveling about four hundred feet above the lake. We watched as Eagle swooped down at tremendous speed. Knowing where his shadow fell, eagle did not alarm the world below the sky, the world below the water.

---

3 Indians view time from this point of reference. "Time" and "being on time" are perimeters they now live in, yet not of their own making. Brother Snake, as he sheds his old Self and moves on into new time, parallels how Native Americans throw off time. If an Indian is on his way to an appointment and meets a friend on the way, his value system dictates that the friend become the priority and the appointment now secondary. Sharing is more important than time or punctuality. To Indians it is known as Indian time. This implies one cannot be late. Everything begins when everything is ready to begin, not when it was scheduled to begin.

Then, with talon flicked, he plucked a large fish out of the water twenty yards from our rowboat. Eagle taught us the execution of presence and precision that day. Learn from Eagle.

Catch the present, as the eagle catches the fish. Connect to the moment and what is happening now.

Indians not only experience events differently, they record events differently. If there is an Indian and a non-Indian watching a horse walk across the field and you ask the Indian what he sees, he will say, "I see a horse walking across the field." The non-Indian will also report the same. However, if you ask them the next day what they saw, the non-Indian will report, "I saw a horse walking across the field." Whereas the Indian will reply, "In my mind I see a horse walking across the field." The past remains in the present.

Let these stories be a reminder for you to keep all things in the present. Like the snake, shed the constraints of time and honor the timeless participants of the Sacred Hoop. Where there is no beginning and no end, there is no time, there is no urgency. Value the members of the Sacred Hoop and your heart will touch other hearts. And like the eagle, focus on the task at hand in order to make it to the top of your mountain.

The Medicine Wheel has been used to identify life stages and cycles. It has also been a guide for balance. Without balance, you are like a deer on ice. Balance is Sacred, and it is also demanding. Be strong. Accept help. Come to balance. Hear what you must. Listen to the demands of your own heartbeat, as you follow the story of this Medicine Wheel:

The Story of Summer Wind

The girl picked up the stone left from the great ice sheets of long ago. The Mishomis she held was smooth and fit her small palm, as perfect as a bird in its nest. She closed her eyes and simply felt its hard gentleness. She knew she could not let it stay

on the beach alone. It belonged to her. Just as she
now belonged to this Mishomis.

Her grandfather was far behind her. He walked
slowly. Now she could run swiftly. As she looked
at his shape approach she remembered how hard it
was to keep up with his long strides when she was
smaller. "Why did life change so much?" she
wondered. "Why can't he run like me, now? We
will never be able to walk side-by-side again," she
thought.

"I'll wait for you, Grandfather," she called to him,
holding the stone tightly in her fist. She sat down
on the warm sand and listened to the waves'
rhythm of the Universe. With her Mishomis,
Summer Wind began to draw pictures of birds, the
sun, of flowers and fish in the sand. All around her
were pictures of the treasures in her heart.

"Ah ho, Summer Wind, I see you have kept your
Mishomis busy remembering the things of the
past," her grandfather smiled as he neared her
sand drawings. "Tell me, what is it that you do not
know how to draw?"

Summer Wind squinted up toward Sun and
thought long and hard. "I really do know most of
what there is to know," she thought. "I know the
world around me, I can even take care of the
babies back at the village."

Remembering how she waited for him, she said,
"Well, I do not understand, Grandfather, why it is
you must grow old."

Her grandfather smiled at her question and sat down. Calling her over to him, she watched as his weathered finger drew a big circle in the sand. "Good. It is my turn to wait for you, as you try to understand."

He pointed to the East side on his circle and traced it gently with his finger. "This is where you entered the world, Summer Wind, and see how you have grown to the South. But, I am lucky, I have traveled the path you now take and have even experienced the West direction." His fingers traced the hoop with tenderness and at each direction, memories of years gone by filled his heart, and blazed through his eyes. "Soon it will be my turn to enter the North direction which leads to the Great Mystery."

Summer Wind looked up at her grandfather. His face smiled deep wrinkles. "He is happy to be old," she thought. Summer Wind had known of the Four Directions all her life. Still, right then, sitting with her grandfather on the sand, the directions came alive. Summer Wind and her grandfather were the directions, there on the sand. But still to grow old, frightened and saddened Summer Wind.

"North is the greatest door to pass through, an honor and part of the cycle of life. Without old age, there is no Sacred Hoop. Without death there can be no life," he said, as though reading her thoughts.

"But there is more to the wheel of life for you to learn." Grandfather traced the Four Directions through the Great Circle. "Notice how the wheel is balanced. Remember your mind, your body, your feelings, and your spirit, Summer Wind. Each is part of you, like the directions of the wheel. Remember to keep it all in balance."

Then he touched the very top of the circle. "This, my sweet child, is the past." Touching the very bottom, he continued, "This is the future. Only give your attention to the past and future during the sunrise and the sunset, for that is the time to remember and to plan. The sun helps us remember our mistakes from the day gone by, and then helps us to set our own sun trail for life." His large hand rested in the center of the circle. Then patting the warm sand he continued, "This is the day. Here is where you must train your mind, body, spirit and emotions. Live most of your time here, in the now, for that is all you really have."

The smiling man then pointed to the East saying, "This is for play. Connect to this child even when you are old and white, like me," he said gently tugging her thick braid.

Moving to the South direction he said, "This is about the inside of you. Focus on your Self to grow and become. Never lose sight of your uniqueness."

Then to the West. "This is for work. Work to contribute. Work for balance."

Grandfather slowly pointed north and added, "And this is for others. Give to others the gifts you are given. Think of the WE, rather than the ME."

"Balance all these, and you will live to smile when the North Door approaches, for you will have lived well. You will have lived your own full life."

"But what about my drawings? Where do they belong?" the girl asked, looking behind her where she had sketched.

"Ah, they belong alongside you on the hoop, just as you drew them. For you travel life together."

"And what about The Great Spirit, Grandfather? Where does the Great Spirit sit?"

"Where do you think?" he asked instead.

Without a word, Summer Wind kissed her Mishomis good-bye and gently placed it in the center of the wheel, knowing they would find each other again. Together, the girl and the grandfather walked side-by-side back through their footprints in the sand.

Look to the Medicine Wheel's Four Directions and to Earth Mother and Father Sky. Look to the center, where God exists in the Now. There are an infinite number of stories for you to hear. They will help you balance the seventh direction: you.

See how birds fly as one with others.
Feel Earth Mother awaken with new life in the
    Spring.
Hear the sound of Wind Spirits sing the songs
    of change.
Wonder why Brother Wolf can run so long.

Practice learning as trees practice growing.
Ask why Bear's tail is short.
Cry with the clouds' tears.
Laugh with the flowers' dance of life.
Reach for the stars.
Remember the Mishomis.
Splash through the puddles.
Follow the birds southern flight when Cousin
    North Wind blows.
Look to see why Beetle's wings are transparent.

It is time for the seventh direction. Design your own Medicine Wheel and write a plan to bring yourself into balance. Be complete and realistic. Balance yourself mentally, physically, emotionally, spiritually, inner world and outer world, work and play, five percent in the past, five percent in the future and ninety percent in the present.

Allow the color of your Self to come through as you focus your attention on the Medicine Wheel's teaching. Feel the expansive wonder of your Self and the world around you.

Color your face with Dandelion.
Laugh along with Loon.
Sing with Vireo.
Set goals with Sun.
Reflect with Waters.
Stretch with Wind.
Work with Beaver.
Cry with Clouds.

Do all this in the now, balanced in your Self.

Above all, reach with the Love of Ain-dah-ing to touch other beating hearts.

PART FOUR

YOUR HEART BEATS STRONG

Brother Eagle soars just to soar,
As Running Deer must run.
Pine Tree reaches for the Light
Gifted by Grandfather Sun.

MEDICINE BAG

I place my heart inside you.

Do you remember the days of kindergarten and show and tell, when you brought your worlds to school inside brown grocery bags? At six years old, you were allowed to collect your identity and encouraged to feel the pride of your Self. Reaching in to pull out your treasures became a sacred ceremony.

As children, you reached in your brown paper bags for the glory of your Self, held high. It was the mystery that only you understood. The pulse of the bag opening connected to the pulse of your heart. Your young heart beat strong with the wondrous excitement of the prized Self. From this understanding and becoming of Self, you shared your essence with others.

As you grew older, show and tell ended. The brown bags were no longer allowed at school. You may even have been told not to color outside the lines, to keep the mud outside, to keep your Kool-Aid smile outside. To become an adult. Keep your toys at home. Keep your Self at home.

The celebration of becoming was denied. Many lost their wonder and their pride in the process. The balance was disturbed.

Native Americans have long understood bag-wisdom. The Medicine Bag is a tradition of collecting, honoring, and engaging your identities.

Years ago, the Medicine Bag was essential to carry Mash-ka-wisen, inner strength, as Indians traveled long distances. The power of one's Medicine Bag is perhaps even more meaningful today than it was long ago. Listen, now, with your sharp ear to this story...

The Medicine Bag

As night accompanied the whippoorwill's song, the traveler watched the woods darken as Grandfather Sun's eyes began to close. With the falling light, it began to rain. At first it was only a soft misting rain, then the drops grew cold and hard. Walking through a curtain of water, the brave pushed on. Colder and colder, the rain turned to sleet. It wasn't long before ice gripped the forest floor. His breath made its own little clouds in front of his quickened pace. The air grew colder.

"Where will I sleep?" the young man wondered, as the ice bit his fingertips. "I cannot lay down here, for I may die." So, the brave continued on.

Each step stole a portion of this young man's stamina, once his pride. Each forward movement pulled on the cramping that stabbed his stomach. The more he clutched at his need for food, the harder it was to continue. As the icy rain ignored his shivers, his feet begged only to be warm and dry. It was all a struggle, an effort to continue.

"I must close the distance between my loved ones and me. I must go on," he repeated to the rhythm of his heart. He touched the buck skin bag tied to his pants and moved on.

His eyes worked to let in as much of the dimming light as possible. The forest was almost one color now: a dark, dark, gray. Trees were no longer trees. They towered over him as shadows—shadows that blended into one Great Shadow. They embodied his fear and surrounded him, engulfed him. The trees became his fear.

The fear tried to trick him, reaching down to confront his Mash-ka-wisen. Fear strove to become his master as it whispered, "Lie down. Let the rain wash you. Let the shadows become your blanket. Let the shadows become your blanket."

Just as the brave thought it might be good to rest, a wolf howled nearby. Four more times the howl was heard, then the rest of the pack joined in. As Brother Wolf sang of endurance, the brave gripped his pouch and connected to his Mash-ka-wisen. Brother Wolf's Mash-ka-wisen merged with his own. Mash-ka-wisen loosened fear's hold and guided his feet further.

The path widened and there in the midst of his fear, under the arms of the trees, the brave found a gift of shelter.

With quiet heart, the grateful brave entered the empty wigwam. Its roof of cedar and walls of birch bark became the womb of Earth Mother. Inside this shelter of bent and tied saplings, the young man

found a fuel bundle, hides for blankets, pine
boughs for a bed, and some roots and jerky.

A smile of many years lit up the shelter as he lit
the fuel bundle. The small pit fire began to warm
the brave as his gratitude began to warm his spirit.
He covered his drying body with the hide robes
and ate the provisions.

Soon the brave was ready to open his Medicine
Bag, but first a ritual of purification was necessary.
The man put tobacco down to thank Earth Mother
for her gifts. Then he lit some sage and, smudging
himself, said, "Cleanse me, Great Spirit. My body
still remembers the fear. My heart remembers its
hurry."

Next, the brave smudged himself with sweet grass
and his spirit sang the Good Song. Lastly, he
sprinkled cedar over the fire and his heart danced
with the familiar snaps and pops. Its full scent
carried his prayers up into Sky Father. "Please,
Spirit Guides, join me." And then with respectful
care, the man opened his Medicine Bag.

Just as the gifted shelter lodged him, his buckskin
Medicine Bag lodged his heart's attachments.
Inside he looked to see his mother's ring, his
father's bowstring, his grandfather's flint stone, his
daughter's beaded hairpiece, and his son's first
arrowhead. The brave's affinity with Brother Wolf
also inhabited the bag, embodied in its eye tooth.
His wife's lock of hair, his grandmother's healing
stone, and other minerals and feathers had also

made the journey. They, too, had followed his trail, just as the sun follows the sky.

And as he reached into his Medicine Bag, the objects released their spirits. The spirits reached out for him. All were present in the lodge, in the Now, with him. The brave's fear had retreated. His Self became WE. And his loneliness was filled with relation.

"Migwetch," the brave whispered, surrounded with hides, boughs, and contentment.

As he put his head down on the skin, where the moment of total satisfaction lives, the spirits heard the beating of his heart. And in the silence between his pulse, the brave heard the eternal beat of the drum.

YOUR MEDICINE BAG

It is time for you to make your own Medicine Bag and tap into your own Mash-ka-wisen. Go now and find what has meaning in your life. What articles represent your loves, your interests, your affinities? What items release the essence of someone no longer with you? What memories do you cherish? What gifts were you given? When you touch these things, what do you feel?

There are many kinds of Medicine Bags for many different purposes. The bag I speak to is your personal bag. To keep its power, it needs to be kept personalized by reserving its contents only for yourself and the privileged disclosure of intimate relationships. In doing this, you give yourself permission to fully know yourself.

IDENTITY

The Medicine Bag helps us to collect our identity. We must go further, however, and come to know our strengths, weaknesses, character defects, our light side and our dark side.

The following pages will escort you through your shadows and lighted places. You will learn how to 1) truly know yourself, 2) discipline yourself, 3) be yourself, and 4) give of yourself. These four principles will guide you in identifying your items for your personal Medicine Bag. You will discover your affinities to support your balance. These items serve as pressure points for spiritual connections.

Know Yourself

Socrates advised: "Know yourself."

Prepare a space for the next two exercises. Find a place of quiet where there will be no distractions. Fill it with only yourself. This is for you. You deserve to know yourself.

Strengths and Weaknesses

I suggest that you draw a line down the center of a blank sheet of paper. On one side of the page list your strengths. On the other side list your weaknesses. This actual recording will allow you to see your Self more clearly. This is a ready reference, a black and white balanced look at you. Take your time. Give yourself the gift of time.

Notice your worth, your assets. Notice your strengths. Celebrate your Self. Open up to the joy it brings you. Be generous in your attention to it. Give to it what you deserve. Embrace your gifts. From this view of yourself, you will see what you can rely on, what you can practice and polish, what you can further become.

Now, study your weaknesses. Look at them. Explore what is under that, and what is under the "that" which you just discovered. It demands your honesty, your willingness to embrace the uncomfortable fear that waits to master you. Face it. From this vantage point you will identify areas that you need to work on.

Values

Please take this time, now, and find your value.

List the top ten things you value most in your life. Your God, spouse, children, job, home, car, nature, computer, TV, or whatever. Then one by one, give them up, sacrifice each for the rest. Continue this until you are down to only one item. You are probably finding that the choices get more difficult the further you go. In other words, you are measuring and prioritizing your value system. Although this may be difficult and even painful, it is very valuable for us to have a well thought out value system.

Spend some time with yourself.
Get acquainted with yourself.
No distractions.
No excuses.

You may find you're in good company when you're alone. One of the greatest tragedies in life is to go through a lifetime, in the same body, with the same Self, and never get to know yourself. How sad.

Take the time to do the two above exercises. Take the time to find your values and who you are.

Discipline Yourself

Cicero advised, "Discipline yourself."

Once you get to know yourself, then you need to discipline yourself in order to get a grip on your inner controls. When you discipline yourself, you learn to become your own responsible authority. You learn to become responsive, rather than being reactive. Instead of knee-jerk, thoughtless behavior, you use time to become. And you become what you think about. You learn to take care of yourself through discipline.

When I first became sober eighteen years ago, I made my own list and discovered my inadequacies and my weaknesses. One by one, I wrote them on one side of an old oilcloth poker chip. On the other side of each poker chip, I wrote the remedy. On one side I wrote arrogance, on the other side, humility. One side indicated defiance, the other side compliance. I carried one of these chips in my pocket at all times. Whenever I reached in, I touched the chip and was reminded to discipline myself. Both my weakness and the antidote was at my fingertips. Each time I touched the chip, I had a decision to make, a choice to engage. At the beginning of the next month, I would rotate the poker chips until I had greatly reduced and even extinguished my weaknesses. Try it. It works, if you work it.

Discipline.
Discipline.
Discipline.

Realize that this includes all of the areas of your Medicine Wheel. All of the areas of your life. Now that you've identified your areas of imbalance or weakness, make the decision to balance it. But this decision must come from you, not your boyfriend, girlfriend, spouse, child, or friend. It must be your decision to discipline.

Be Yourself

Freud advised, "Be yourself."

To be yourself is to experience life. That's what it's all about. Find the courage to be yourself, not a clone, not an expectation, not a programmed robot. Be uniquely yourself. There is no one like you. There never was, nor will there ever be another you.

Learn just to be. Free yourself from others. Free yourself from your expectations. Free yourself from "shoulds." Free your Self.

It is an ongoing process of be-coming. It requires courage to face life as it is. Remember what the Navajo says. "What is, is." A deer in the woods does not stare at the bear and wish it were the bear. It is fully content being itself. The turtle does not envy the frog, nor the frog envy the bird.

Follow your directives

Take what you've found out about who you are, what you now know. Follow those directives. If you found that you prefer fried onions, fry them. If you found you love music, dance. If you found you need quiet, be alone. If you found you love your children, spend time with them. If you found you do not like your job, find a new one. Whatever you found - be it! If it takes discipline, then discipline yourself. If it is easy, then relax and enjoy. But do it. Be it. Become it.

You are responsible to the Universe to be who you are meant to be. If you are scared because it is a new way to be, do it anyway. If you say, "I can't," tap your Mash-ka-wisen and say, "I can!" If you shake and shudder at the thought of being who you really are, then shake and shudder. You will not break. Take the risk and flap your own wings. Be who you are.

Be yourself, express yourself, and enjoy the experience. That's what we're here for and that's all there is. Go for it all, make a total commitment to becoming.

Give of Yourself

Jesus advised, "Give to Caesar what is Caesar's, and give to God what is God's."

This addresses both the spiritual realms and the natural realms, recognizing that they are each the opposite sides of the same thing. The Spirit World needs attention and the natural world needs attention. Keep a foot in both realms. Give to each. Jesus said, "Give of yourself." Once you have become yourself, you have something to give... yourself.

The Indian way is "WE." This is a giving system. The women are in the center, or the hub of the wheel, because they create and nurture new life. The men are at the periphery, supporting the center. All work together for the common "WE." They are the bees in a beehive, where their effort is for the common welfare of the entire hive. It is an effort of giving. On your journey to becoming, find what you have to give, then offer it freely. Look to your list. What are your strengths? The longer this list is, the greater is your obligation to the Sacred Hoop. Recognize that what you give is for the good of all.

What is your talent? Share it with others.

What is your strength? Give it to others.

What is your passion? Reveal it to others.

What is your understanding? Teach it to others.

Once a day, be deliberate in the act of giving. Choose how and what you will give. Discipline yourself to do this each day, and soon you will be living a giving life. Give only for the sake of giving. In solitude, give. In the presence of others, give. You take much from this world. Like the brave, you must place your tobacco down and give the world something back.

COLLECT YOURSELF

Your Medicine Bag may contain the items that best represent the YOU on this journey to Self. They are items that represent who you really are, what you really are connected to, your Primary Essence. They are items that help you on the path to disciplining yourself. They are items that encourage you to be you. They are items that you now can give to others. They are the gifts of yourself.

In your weakest moments you need to collect yourself, so that all aspects of yourself come into the center hub of the Medicine Wheel. You can collect your identity and energies in your Medicine Bag. As you go through life you can add items to your bag, or you can eliminate something. For life has a way of bringing certain people, places, and things into your life for certain periods of time and then you separate in different directions. So, too, with the Medicine Bag, certain items are effective for a certain amount of time. Some energies remain lifelong and some are of temporary support. Allow the contents of your Medicine Bag to be fluid. If they lose their potency, don't stay stuck—discard them and find an expression of a new source.

What is important is that you connect with the spiritual energies without getting stuck on the items.

Devise your own ritual to open your Medicine Bag. Make it a meaningful invitation for the spirits to join you. When you are feeling depressed, lonely, or disconnected, you will find your energy source and essence within your Medicine Bag. The Medicine Bag will help to ground you to your spiritual center. Hear Black Elk's wisdom as he points out that the spiritual center of the Universe, or the most holy mountain top, is within every individual and not on some mountain peak.

The Medicine Bag goes far beyond its contents. It enlists all energies just as your breath connects you to all people. Chief Seattle taught that man belongs to Earth. Earth does not belong to Man. Love the land as the newborn child loves his mother's heartbeat.

Come to know that the Spirit World will respond if you approach it humbly and earnestly. Ask the Spirit World what it expects of you, what its will is for you. Then expect the spirit powers to transfer their powers to you as you carry out that expectation. Become the servant of the Spirit World as the mother bird serves the needs of her brood.

Return to the sound of Earth Mother's heartbeat. Notice how the sapling practices the whisper of its Parent Pine. Hear the rehearsal of the eaglets' wings learning to fly. Listen to the water babble over pebbles, as it trains itself to rush down the side of a mountain.

What does your heart practice? What are you becoming? Always, there are choices. What you choose to practice, you are choosing to become. It is that simple.

We have another Medicine Bag. It is eternally internal. Tears and laughter are its contents. They are the best medicine for releasing stress and tension. Use these medicines freely to be fully alive. Become proficient with both. Both medicines are there to help you heal any trauma. Learn to use your medicines well, for they are there to keep you healthy.

Your Medicine Bag is what you choose to put in it, what you choose to value, what you choose to practice, what you choose to listen to.

Listen to the silence between the beats. Notice the is and the is not. There are always two ways to look at the same thing. Your weaknesses can become your strengths. Your tears can become your joy.

Think of the Here and the There. You are free to move wherever you need, to go wherever you must. The path you are now on (here), will become only a memory (there) as you travel to your next wigwam. It is all so temporary. All things pass with time. All pain, all suffering, waits for time to take them there—away from your here.

Realize that the contents of your Medicine Bag are only limited by your choices and your actions. Engage your Medicine Bag, your Mash-ka-wisen, your own inner strength. By doing so, you will be able to leave your gifts for the next traveler in the forest. You will be able to prepare a wigwam for them. You will be able to give the gift of healing, as you have healed yourself.

> I place my heart inside you.
> My love is nestled here.
> I touch the stone that healed me.
> I feel my mother near.

I place the gifts once given
Inside your soft embrace.
I feel the wings of sparrow hawk
Circle in my empty space.

I place my dreams inside you.
My goals, my hopes, and fears.
I feel your power fill me.
I bless you with my tears.

I place myself inside you,
My memories of days gone by.
I thank you for your opening.
You give me wings to fly.

BIMADISIWIN

"Bimadisiwin is the good life,"
the Elder answered.

Riding along with my Grandpa in his cream and forest green Packard, he turned to me and said, "If this road had one more curve in it, it would be straight."

He seemed so wise when I was five years old. I knelt up to see over the walnut dash board and my eyes followed the curves in the road. I pictured a snake slithering, curving, and becoming straight. "He's right," I said to myself. "Just one more curve *would* make this road straight."

When I grew older I laughed at this idea. Away from childhood, I closed my ears to his wisdom and heard only the ridiculous thoughts of an old man.

Many years made my own road curvy. Preoccupied with "living," I had forgotten what true living was. Then, sobriety offered me a new vantage point and revealed the effects of my life choices. Many curves of joy and pain, of hard work and selfishness, of give and take had paved my life. The most painful of all illnesses, alcoholism, had cut the deepest. Under its power, I had injured myself and others. I had lived mostly for ME. There were many amends to make. Many bridges to repair.

From sunrise to sunset, I had logged miles of woods, worked in hot factories, drove truck, and yet had avoided responsibility. I had cared for an injured horse, but mostly I cared for myself. I had given my coat to someone in need, but still hoarded my alcohol. My life was not in balance. It was off center. It was more ME than WE.

I returned to the Old Age wisdom of my people and learned to collect my identity in a Medicine Bag. Recognizing my personal connection to the Universe, Mitakuye-Oyasin, I began to see with soft eyes. Connecting to my Ain-dah-ing, I realized that inside Grandpa's statement, there was the white light of wisdom. Here I found my inner strength, my Mash-ka-wisen, to start again.

New possibilities now existed on my road of curves, and I learned that it would take Purpose to pull my curves straight. Grandpa's curvy road was so close to becoming straight. It could have been, if only. And how many times, have I said to myself, "If only, I'd..." or "If only..."

The "If only's" are not spoken by those who live their Bimadisiwin[1], their own full life. The caterpillar does not say, "If only I could fly." It becomes and then flies. The stone does not say, "If only I could be soft." It collapses into softness. Just as you, too, will fly and will collapse into your softness. The power is within you. The ability to make your road straight is within your reach. Bimadisiwin teaches you how.

Bimadisiwin means to live life in the fullest sense: to experience, to dance your dance, to express your Self. The Spirit World is your home, but the natural world is your home away from home. This world prepares you for your return. So, embrace Bimadisiwin and live fully, expand your ability to experience the bliss of the spiritual dimension. Find Ain-dah-ing, your home within your heart, and then connect to the Spirit World. It will expand your wonder of this natu-

---

[1] Pronounced: be-ma-DEE-zee-win

ral dimension. Both sides of consciousness (spirit world and natural world) emphasize, expand, and illuminate the other.

FATE, FREE WILL, AND PURPOSE

Bimadisiwin encompasses 1) fate, 2) free will, and 3) purpose. Living fully requires an appreciation of all three of these concepts. They may appear contradictory, yet they hold hands with one another. They follow the same beat of the eternal circle, the Sacred Hoop. Fate, free will, and purpose need each other to complete the hoop.

Fate

Fate is the expression of the Spirit World's intent, desire, and directional input. The Spirit World chooses to have people, places, and things come in and out of our lives. Think of times in your life that coincidence knocked on your door. Reflect on the importance that one person has made in your life direction. Hear the song that played through the winds of change, as you changed because of your changed environment. Constantly connecting, then separating, the dance of life follows the Sacred Hoop, with the guidance of fate.

Free Will

We are the architects of the temporal side of our life. Our destiny in the natural dimension is a matter of choices, decisions, options, and alternatives. Our actions or lack of action (which is also a decision) will determine our circumstance. Free will has its own echo effect, as fate plays out its role. Free will plays its own rhythm, and a syncopation of the two beats results. I chose to drink and I lost respect. I now choose to heal and I respect myself. Constantly we make choices and live with the consequences of those choices. Life is a series of choices. Choose to know. Choose to discipline. Choose to be. Choose to give.

Purpose

Each individual has a special purpose. Go within the Self, to the source of the Self, to your Primary Essence, to find and see your purpose. Use your mind's eye to look with objective wonder. The connection to this big idea for your life, your purpose, is a wonderful experience. It is exciting. A life with purpose makes your heart beat strong. It creates a bigger appetite for bigger living. It grows. Stronger and stronger, your heart continues to beat, does not skip a beat, and can be heard by others as your presence radiates your purpose. Choices become adventures. Hurdles become challenges. Setbacks become learning experiences.

You begin to hear Life's questions once you have found your purpose and can hear your own heart beat strong. It will test your Mash-ka-wisen and strengthen your character. Purpose is Life's yellow highlighter. It emphasizes fate and directs your free will. It is like the water that you drink: it both nourishes your life and becomes a river for connections to be made. Drink, now, of the spiritual well and find the purpose that will nourish your fate and guide your free will.

THE FULL LIFE

Bimadisiwin is demanding. It is also rewarding. Listen to your heart as you run. It beats strong. Your heart will accommodate your aspirations and expectations. Your heart will provide the energy. Your body will provide the vehicle. Your mind will provide the vision. Your spirit will provide the Mash-ka-wisen.

Listen carefully to Self, to others, and to the Spirit World. You hear many things when you are in alignment with them. You can hear the squawking of the blabber-mouth blue jay, as well as the faint whispers and mental intents of the Spirits offering thoughts you could never have concluded on your own. Oneness magnifies the volume of the silent Spirit World. Oneness opens you to your own Bimadisiwin, to the fullness of your life.

Learn the lesson of the acorn. How does an acorn know to become an oak tree? Because it yields to itself, accepts itself, so that it can become itself, in order to experience itself.

Yield.

Accept.

Become.

Experience.

The acorn yields to the forces, falls quietly from Sky Father and penetrates Earth Mother's womb. The acorn is activated as it accepts its new environment. Earth, sky, sun, rain, night, all work together to nurture and shape acorn as it grows into a sapling, then an adolescent, then an adult. Once acorn has achieved its genetic programming and potential growth, it can become its fullest sense of Self. It experiences the circumference of Earth Mother's body, like a squealing child that feels that the more of mother's body he can touch, the more love he will receive. Fate, free will, and purpose are experienced by the acorn.

Remember, too, the mightiest oak was once a nut. There's an encouraging thought.

Like the acorn nut, you need to crack your shell so your essence can emerge. Trust the Universe to nurture, guide, and support you, like the acorn trusts its Mother and Father. The Spirit World will support you as you reach toward Grandfather Sun to grow into your own experience. Can you see that the acorn trusts the Universe? And the Universe trusts the acorn to fulfill itself? Trust yourself. Have faith in yourself and in the Universe.

TRUST IN THE UNIVERSE

Sitting on a small stump outside our cabin door, I learned about trust. Moccasin Mike and Grandpa were my teachers. On the outside counter that looked like a fish-cleaning board, Grandpa would place his straight razor next to his mug of shaving soap, water, and towel. Then he'd get out the razor strap and I would become mesmerized by the beautiful rhythm of the razor being sharpened on the strap. It was a ceremony. Grandpa and Moccasin Mike were the participants, and I was the observer. Grandpa would continue the rhythm until he could feel the sharpness with his mind. Without fail, Mike would then hold a piece of birch bark in front of me and Grandpa would slide the razor delicately down the front of the bark, shredding the Indian paper easily with its gentle sharpness. It was only then that my eyes would see the sharpness they had both sensed. Then the lathering would begin, and one would brush the soapy lather on the other. As gently as the birch bark was cut, each would shave the face of his friend. Truly, an exercise in trustworthiness!

These two Elders were free to "be" with one another. My grandfather, a wealthy logger and Moccasin Mike, an impoverished logger, connected not to each other's status, but to their state of being. They were able to find the best part of one another. They enjoyed life immensely and yielded to life circumstances.

Yield and you will "be" as you were meant to be.

Be your truest Self and seek your truest passion. Find what pleases you. Find what grabs you. I enjoy doing what I do... psychotherapy, simultaneously guiding the conscious and unconscious areas of the mind into synchronicity and alignment. That's my bag. That's my talent. That's my gift. That's my thing.

Why? Because the Spirit World chose my fate. I accepted my free will and I confirmed my purpose. We confirm our purpose through an inner sense of conviction, completion, fulfillment, joy, and sufficiency. We are in alignment and harmony with our purpose when we experience an inner state of joy, which is our bench mark and validation.

What is your joy? What is your purpose?

Find it.
Confirm it.
Be it.
Then give it away.

One of the greatest spiritual laws of the Universe is, "if you want to keep it, you must give it away." This paradox, like other spiritual secrets, speaks to the WE rather than to the ME.

THE VISION QUEST

The story of the vision quest speaks directly to the beating of Bimadisiwin. Listen and you will hear how fate, free will, and purpose beat as one:

> The sky was a beautiful explosion of color. Grandfather Sun's setting reached out with each dimming color to remind Little Otter that the power of the Universe awaited his recognition. Little Otter hoped his heart would soon discover his fate. He wanted to join the Great Heartbeat with the rhythm of his purpose. Little Otter shuffled his feet in the rich soil and wondered with great anticipation what purpose would be shown to him. At fourteen, this quest for a vision was expected, was necessary. His eldest brother was the great hunter. His friend was learning to be a healer. Little Otter was ready. He wanted to discover his Self. He needed to return to his Ain-dah-ing, to hear the voice of the Great Silence.
>
> In the fading magenta of the night sky, the words and the non-words of his Medicine Guide became a trance of purpose-finding. The monotone beseeching of the spirits blended with the sky colors and encircled Little Otter with the importance of his vision quest. Each moment of the entrance ceremony echoed in the silence between Little Otter's heartbeat, the importance of it all flowed

out from him. And he felt big. Bigger than he had ever felt before. Inside his heart, Little Otter smiled a big smile, but hid it from his Medicine Guide. He looked to the vision pit dug into Earth Mother[2]. This was too important and solemn an occasion to let his emotions overflow into the moment. Soon he would be able to be someone. Someone like his brother. Someone like his friend.

Little Otter kept his eyes low and disciplined his thoughts to focus only on the words being spoken and the magnitude of what was ahead of him. He would follow the sun trail into the west and enter the pit. He would discover the spirit connection of his own essence. He would find his purpose. Crawling into the vision pit, Little Otter's body filled the hole made for him. The cool earth held him as his body remembered Earth Mother.

The last light was extinguished like the flame of a candle, as his Medicine Guide pulled the skin tarp over the pit that became Little Otter's womb. With only a blanket and a sacred pipe, Little Otter had left the world of light, sound, and food, to enter the world within.

It wasn't long before Little Otter's quiet spirit asked the Creator what he needed to become. He waited patiently, knowing the Creator would speak in silence and outside of time.

---

[2] Some vision quests were conducted on mountain tops, high places, or by a waterfall.

He waited all that night. He waited throughout the next day. He waited until he thought he could wait no more. Little Otter asked again, to be sure the Great Spirit had heard him. But still he heard nothing.

After the end of the first day, when night had made its full circle, the corner of the skin covering the night sky was lifted. Little Otter's Medicine Guide had come to check on him and asked, "Have you listened to the Drum? Do you know what purpose beats for you?"

Little Otter, growing weak and mentally exhausted from his first day, only shook his head. Yet a hint of hope was still visible on his face and he said, "It will come to me." Assuring himself more than his Guide he whispered, "My purpose will come."

Yet two more nights circled. Dreams of Brother Wolf filled the cool darkness of his earthen bed. And each night his Medicine Guide came and asked him, "Did you hear the beating of the Drum?"

And each time Little Otter answered, "It will come. My purpose will come." Little Otter grew weak. He was losing himself inside Earth Mother. He began to doubt.

Great hunger and an even greater appetite to leave his pit began to empty Little Otter of his hope. There was no purpose in the vision pit. There was no Bimadisiwin. There was only loneliness, pain, and his dreams. Three days of this great emptying had only filled Little Otter with dreams of wolf songs. "Useless dreams," Little Otter thought. "I need to hear the song of my Creator, not the songs of Brother Wolf."

On the fourth night, Little Otter's Medicine Guide, once again came to check on him.

"Little Otter, have you heard the power of the Drum? Have you listened to the Spirit World?"

"There is no purpose for me!" Little Otter cried out. "The only sound I hear is the sound of Brother Wolf."

"You can leave if there is nothing for you. The choice is always yours," his Medicine Guide said.

Still the boy chose to stay and the flap remained Little Otter's lowered sky.

That night, the dreams of Brother Wolf returned. Little Otter saw through wolf eyes a run through darkened woods. He heard the beating of the wolf's heart ahead of the forest sounds. He felt the wolf's breath go in and out with quiet endurance, cool then warm, cool then warm.

"You can leave if there is nothing for you," he heard his Guide echo in his dream.

"But what is here for me?" he cried. "I can only see through wolf eyes, I can only hear through wolf ears. I can only feel through the breath of my brother wolf."

"Yes," spoke the wolf with the voice of his Medicine Guide. "You can understand the language others can not hear. You can see the things others can not see. You can feel the breath others can not feel."

Little Otter lifted his own cover of doubt and saw his purpose. He was to release the visions of his tribal brothers. He was to be himself. He was always there. He was to show others the woods through the eyes of the wolf. To speak the language of nature. To feel the heartbeat of all of life. To share this knowledge with others. To teach like the wolf.

Then a Great Silence filled Little Otter's dream, until even the dream was silent.

The Spirit World spoke into the silence, touched Little Otter with the feathers of understanding, and illuminated the Great Light within.

Whose life are you really trying to live? How can you live your life as fully as possible? What is your vision?

Find the time needed to reflect on your life circumstances, your *fate*. Use your *free will* and choose ways to help you become yourself. Look at the curves in your road and discover what *purpose co*uld pull it straight. Give yourself the gift of time to uncover your own blinders. See the changes needed for your life. Then, live these changes, become these changes, and you will live Bimadisiwin.

Come and experience the change from within. Like Little Otter open up to the power of the Spirit World through a reflective process of Self. Gitchi Manidoo awaits to show your vision's direction, but you must choose to hear the voice of the Spirit World. You must choose to do what it takes to fulfill your purpose. You must spend time in your own Ain-dah-ing and lift the covers you use to hide the real you, the light of your truest Self. Like Little Otter, find what is keeping you from hearing the Great Pulse. The information gained from the center of the God's circle will change your inner Self. The ego (ME) will peel off to greater consciousness (WE).

The Creator makes the change, but you must be willing. You need to activate this change with your most precious gift: free will. Through Bimadisiwin you will see yourself in the greater scheme of things. Living a full life gives you a bigger perspective. New values and principles will come to you, and daily annoyances will become less disturbing. As you enter new awakenings, many choices and options will become available. It is the pebble-in-the-water effect of positive focus: the more positive your focus, the more positive your consequences, the more positive your focus. It reverberates from life circle, to life circle, to life circle.

Bimadisiwin grows. You grow. Bimadisiwin grows. Discover what has been in you all the time. Your Primary Essence is connected to the sacred.

As you live Bimadisiwin, a cause-and-effect relationship sustains a wonderful momentum to your life circle. What you believe, you practice and what you practice you become. You believe in your vision of you. You practice this vision. You become this vision.

Look for the rainbow in the puddle, see the colors in the debris, hear the symphony in your own spirit. Then stir the puddle and watch the rainbow reappear. Separate the debris into a rainbow of color. Sing a rainbow song within you. Once you look for ways to believe and practice, you will become the rainbow.

What are you believing? What are you practicing? What are you becoming? It is a matter of choice. See how your curvy road of life needs only one more curve. One more deliberate turn from yourself may, indeed, pull it straight, to it's purpose of being. For this is the seventh direction. The seventh direction is you. You are the road my grandpa spoke of.

Today, I tell my children, as we drive down the curvy lake road, "You know, if this road had one more curve in it, it would be straight." And my children listen to me, to hear my grandpa's wisdom, to hear of the seventh direction.

NAMAJI

At rippled edge of darkened Sky
Bows dignity of Cloud.
Colors honor Setting Sun
Moon and Stars are Proud.

Sacred holds the dark and light
Ant, and Hill and Hawks—
As fire splashes onto Her,
Respectfully she walks.

THE STORY OF NOKOMIS (part one)

She smoothed the white shawl around her shoulders before entering the dance arena. It was a simple movement, like a bird straightening its feathers. Her two hands automatically reached up and pulled gently, yet firmly, until the shawl fell into place. Nokomis was completely aware of her movement. Today, she noticed everything: the cut cedar boughs that laced the frame above the Great

Circle giving shade for the dancers, the laughing
children running tirelessly around the outside of
the dance, the smell from the Sacred Fire down the
path, the grayish purple sky that was getting ready
to set. Mostly, she was aware of the beat, the great
beat of the drum, the connecting beat of her
people.

She had talked and laughed for most of that day,
with her family and friends, aware that the moment of this dance would come, aware of the drum
beat in the background. The beat of Powwow was
the beat of Nokomis' life.

As Nokomis entered the dance ring, she felt all
eyes fixed on her. Her white buck skin dress was
as soft as her steps, her face as smooth as the
gentleness of her heart. This was her dance, her
honor song.

Nokomis entered the ring at East, accompanied by
two head dancers. And with her head held high,
the white eagle feather that adorned her hair
accented her dignified gait. Out of memory, more
than anything else, Nokomis knew all were standing now in her honor. With soft step, the three
began their dance around the Powwow circle.

To Nokomis, this was the Dance of her Life. This
was the summary of everything she had experienced, everything she was. Each time she placed
her soft white moccasin down to massage Earth
Mother, she reconnected with her essence. Each
beat from the drum echoed the beat of her heart.

Each rise of the singers' voice reached the secrets inside her and touched her with honor. This dance was for her.

As Nokomis passed through the East, she envisioned a little girl with long black braids, playing with the delight of a dandelion. She remembered her Elders telling stories and felt her father once again picking her up in his strong arms. The innocent awe of life tickled her. She touched the Medicine Bag that hung from her wrist and whispered, "Migwetch." All was good in the East direction.

Nokomis continued on her Circle to the South and felt the supportive presence of her fellow dancers. The beat of the drum grew faster and stronger and Nokomis followed its story, twirling inside with the energy of youth. The white shawl remembered the wings she once soared with. Nokomis felt her face flush before her family. Her feathered fan cooled her face as the beat continued and the singers sang of the South. All was good in the South direction.

Now, Nokomis looked only before her. The moment was as powerful as any she had known. The beat of the drum, the beat of her heart, the song of her life. She flowed with the current of the Sacred Hoop, circling the great beat, the Source of all Life.

The singers honored her with their song, for they sang of her life, the work and the play, the all of her life.

Reaching the West direction, Nokomis remembered
her husband, young and strong, holding her hand
with a tenderness that only she knew. She felt the
wonder of creation and held her babies one more
time in the shawl that wrapped her arms. She felt
the strength of her giving arms, the filling of their
love. Nokomis saw the seasons of life touch her
with their gifts of joy and pain. She saw her
beauty. All was good in the West direction.

The beat continued as Nokomis continued around
the hoop, feeling her completion nearing, the
completion to where it would all start again.

The beat paused, as did her heart in anticipation of
the North, as it opened to her. Nokomis understood cloud softness, the wonder of the new birth,
the joy of sharing the stories that she had heard in
the East. Now was her time for giving.

Mostly, she felt the emptying. Nokomis felt the
pain of that emptying, remembered her husband
departing, her final kiss on his eyelids as they
closed one last time. She had felt the All of life
experiences. The shawl now distinguished her
white headdress with the gentleness of old age.

She had reached the North. The beat continued
and Nokomis awaited the joy of life with her
escorts, for her vessel of love would now be filled.

Nokomis' daughter entered the dance circle and
hugged her mother with great respect and love.
Dancing with the beat of the drum, she fell in

behind Nokomis, to begin the trail of love. She danced to the beat of the eternal. Nokomis gave her arms to her son, and he honored her with his bright smile and embrace. It was the same smile as the one she had given him the day of his birth.

Family and friends waited patiently in line to greet Nokomis. They anticipated the joy of honoring her. The drum continued to beat and Nokomis graciously accepted all of the tributes that followed, the shaking of hands, the hugs, the kind words of recognition. Nokomis proudly accepted her place in the Sacred Hoop of Life.

The line wound around like a snake, waiting behind the dignity of this woman. The energy increased as all took their place, moving on this Great Circle of Life. The song continued. All danced. The drum pulsed on. Finally, Nokomis moved forward to accept the completion, and the Sacred Hoop became a river, filling and flowing over Nokomis with the greatest of all gifts...love.

RESPECT, HONOR, DIGNITY, AND PRIDE

The highest of all Anishinaabe life principles is called Namaji[1]: respect, honor, dignity, and pride.

Respect, honor, dignity and pride are given and accepted freely. They are the gifts of a true connection to the Spirit World. These are the flowers that bloom of Mitakuye-Oyasin. They are the promising buds on the wreath of Life.

---

[1] Pronounced: NA-MA-GEE.

Like the lily pads in the lake, Namaji unfolds at different levels. Some lilies get less sun, deep down in the water, on their string vine. They are flooded with the rushing concerns of their world. Other lilies get more sun, close to the top of the water, and are able to look out to the other side and see what is possible. Some lily pads lay on top of the water and touch the wonder of a new state of being, while others transcend the water as flower stems, opening to the sunlight of wisdom. As you transcend the depths of your life, you experience Namaji—a higher state of consciousness.

It is time to emerge from the depths of your Self and discover Life's treasure.

Respect

Run your hands through the golden sands of time. Each granule has a story, a purpose, a connection to the sea of Life. Respect and see the sacred in all, the purpose of all, and the connectedness of all. Feel the beauty of Life. Experience the wonder of Life. View the truth from different angles. Let the granules fall through time and thank them for their moment. As part of One, respect all.

Honor

Open up to life and experience life—it is your greatest fortune. You are honored by the all of Life. Life gives you the sand to build your abode. Honor Life by offering your best. Build your life, but also, let it sink back into Earth Mother and become part of Her. Feel the welcome. Watch how the sea of life moves your sands to their rightful place. Honor all granules that touch you on your journey, for they are your roots, your essence.

Dignity

Dignity is Self respect and Self honor. Recognize your role in the sands of time and your dignity will grow. Dignity is the headdress of Life, the blanket of honor and respect. Dignity abides in the home within your heart, yet is connected to Earth Mother. Connect and become a vital participant. Give dignity to all and dignify all of Life. Elevate the sacredness in all. That is how you dignify yourself. Dignity is not your achievement, it is the invisible support of it.

Pride

Pride is the sun's sparkle on the grains of sand. Pride flows from the Sacred Essence and gives you the courage to protect your values. Pride is the radiance of truth, the joy of knowing yourself completely. Pride is a gift you can give your children as you teach them to build their own home within their heart. Pride is connecting to the sea that will wash your life back to its beginning. Pride is embracing the circle of life.

Namaji manifests Mitakuye-Oyasin. It is a sacred code of living. Can you see that an ant, mosquito, squirrel, rabbit, deer, duck, bear and hawk have as much an equal right to life and the environment as we do? We are no more important in the Creator's eye than they are; and we are no less important. All creation is equal. Not man over snake, nor snake over man. All are one and one is all.

As in the honor dance of Nokomis, feel the completion Namaji brings with it. With great respect recognize all are equal. With honor, honor all: the two-legged, four-legged, winged, finned, creepers and crawlers. With dignity, dance. With pride, wear your feathers for all to see.

The dance of Life moves on and we are honored with air to breath, water to drink, and food to eat. We are honored by Grandfather Sun, Grandmother Moon, and the Wind Spirits. They offer us Namaji. What do we offer them?

THE STORY OF NOKOMIS (part two)

It was time for the feast. Nokomis laid out her
cloth on Earth Mother, still full of the dance inside.

Women swarmed the feast area with fry bread,
corn soup, venison, potatoes, cranberries, turkey,
squash, coffee and cake. Soon Earth Mother was
blanketed with Her gifts of food.

Nokomis watched her son make up the first plate.
It was the plate for Earth Mother. He left to feed
Her, placing the dish next to the great pine.

All stood and listened quietly as an Elder offered
the prayer to Gitchi Manidoo. As he placed tobacco[2] down, Nokomis thanked Earth Mother for
the honor, thanked Her for all of life.

The children came to the blanket and began filling
plates with the good food. Each plate was taken to
an Elder.

A child offered Nokomis his plate and smiled shyly
before returning to his seat. Nokomis nodded and
smiled back, for she remembered how she, too,
had once put the cake on top of her Elder's potatoes.

This is Namaji: respect, honor, dignity, and pride. From the East
Direction to the North Direction, the children need the Elders and the
Elders need the children. Namaji is the geyser that lifts all creation to
sacredness. All is elevated and cared for. Namaji beats strong of commitment, responsibility, and accountability. It embraces and nurtures
the WE of this world. Commit to all, become responsible and accountable to all. For all is committed, responsible, and accountable to
you. Namaji is a mutual Life principle.

---

[2] Tobacco is considered the head of all medicines.

RED ROAD

Namaji guides us along the Red Road of life. The Red Road is the Sacred Path for living in harmony with the natural order. Red is the color of our blood. It is the color of the most sacred Indian stone, the pipe stone[3].

We can easily travel from California to New York, driving only at night. The headlights illuminate the dark path before us. That is all we need to see. We focus on a few hundred feet at a time, adding up to thousands of miles. The Red Road, the narrow path between dark and bright, is difficult to follow within the depths of yourself. Follow the soft glow of the Eternal Light and avoid the dark and bright sides[4]. Travel the Sacred Hoop of timelessness into the sunlight of Ain-dah-ing.

Dark is the absence of Light. If we veer off into complete darkness, we punish ourselves because Namaji demands accountability. Consequences for indiscretions are self imposed, for we choose by our actions. Just as the old way was to banish a member from the tribe, so too, are we banished from our inner society if we choose to go off the Red Road into darkness.

The glare of blinding light may also cause us to veer off the Red Road of Life. Complete lightness causes us to become self-righteous, condescending, and judgmental. WE start to believe the light that reflects off us is our own!

An alcoholic who successfully stays sober, walks the Red Road. Without the denial and depression of active alcoholism, he escapes the darkness and the consequences it brings. Without the delusion

---

[3] Pipe stone is a red stone that looks like hardened clay and is used to make sacred pipe bowls.

[4] Virtue and evil are cultures' self-made constructs. What may be evil to one may be virtue to another. The idea of a universal evil, however, is one that goes beyond the confines of this book. In Indian, we say, "Invite the devil to Powwow so you can keep an eye on him." It is best to know where evil and virtue are but not to embrace either.

and grandiosity of self achievement, he is able to avoid the glaring brightness of judgmentalism. By staying sober one beat at a time, he recognizes the gift of his sobriety and his role in this new way of life. By walking the Red Road, he keeps his eye on his lighted path.

Many people try to make life black and white and conveniently fit all experiences in either camp of brightness or darkness. What color is Brother Skunk? If you concentrate on the black, with a hard eye, Skunk is black. If you concentrate on the white stripe, again with a hard eye, Skunk is white. But if you concentrate on the whole of Skunk, with a soft eye, Skunk is gray.

Rarely is Life white or black. Certainly there are wonderfully white moments, as celebrating a birth. Certainly there are tragic black moments, as mourning a death. But even these mountains and valleys are earmarked by the overcast of shadows and the silver lining of clouds. We need to live life, in between the black and the white.

Life is bitter-sweet. For life is not all or nothing. Life is everything on the continuum of experience. Life asks us to feel the fullness of the Red Road, to feel the pain as well as the joy, to feel the anger as well as the forgiveness, to feel the hunger as well as the satisfaction. The blueberries my children picked were both bitter and sweet. The children left the woods not only with blueberry juice all over their faces, but with the dozens of wood ticks that accompanied their sweetness.

Sacredness encompasses the entire experience. Accept even the most painful experiences in life. Thank the wood ticks for their part of the experience. The Sacred Strawberry Road is in between the black and white. It is the narrow path between bright and dark.

When we walk softly on the red path we are peaceful and calm. The heartbeat of life gives our feet the cadence and we joyfully follow the beat. When we feel uneasy, upset, or our emotions cloud our thinking, we are not staying between the ditches of life's road. We need to get back on the Hoop of Life. The ditches are bumpy reminders to get re-centered, re-balanced and reconnected to the Spirit World.

Walk in harmony. Walk in beauty. Don't cling to dark or bright. Look for the rainbow in the puddle, for every negative has within it a positive and vice versa. Be deliberate with your choices and intentions. Follow your heart. Follow your dream beat. Life is a boomerang and will return to you what you send out into the Universe.

Abuse returns abuse. Namaji returns Namaji. Life is circular, it will come full circle. You are the designer of your fortune.

Softly place your moccasin on the Red Road and you will find your joy. Discover how Earth Mother's energy supports you. Walk gently on your Mother's Back and she will embrace your step. Honor Her and She will honor you. Walk with Namaji down the Red Road of Life.

MANIDOO

Manidoo[5] is the word for spirit. Gitchi Manidoo is the word for Great Spirit. Resist the temptation to define the Creator, who is indefinable. The more we try to capture the Creator's essence, the less we understand.

Come to Gitchi Manidoo.

The Great Spirit is love. Pure love. That is our essence. Imagine what a full encounter with divinity would be like. Perhaps you have already experienced the pleasing paralysis a sunrise or sunset can bring. This is a mere reflection of the Great Spirit's awe. We would probably forget to eat, drink, or even move if we beheld this sacredness directly. We would lose total sense of Self, for we would become the container that holds bliss, that is awaiting our return.

In this temporal state, we expand the volume of our spiritual vessel through life's teachings, trials, and tribulations. All these things expand our capacity to contain more bliss when we go home to the Spirit World. Pain gives birth to both the temporal and spiritual. See that all of life experiences are openings for love to enter. We carve our own vessel through life experiences. All are necessary to open us to love.

---

[5] Pronounced: MON-ee-doo

We harmonize with Life by loving. To love all is to see the Divine in all, the sacredness in all, the sacredness in Self. We are of God's essence. We are of love's essence. Look deep into the pool of Self and see what's there. Look deep in the pool of the other and see the Divine. Look deep into the Universe and see the Sacred.

Love is both the essence of the Great Spirit, as well as the Sacred Mystery. Love is the fountain of all creation. As the center of the Medicine Wheel, it is the Great Mystery transformed in this dimension. Love Self and all of life. Rediscover your capability to love in this way. Take this moment and create the most pleasant experience of your life. You are the creator and the recipient. You are both the potter and the vessel of the love experience.

You will see that love is both a cause of greater health, as well as an effect of greater health. One begets the other. But first there must be love.

EARTH

Connect to Manidoo with your spirit, for the spirits are everywhere. Give your time to the timeless and enter Gitchi Manidoo's house. You will find peace and tranquillity where only the Now exists. Here you will rest with quiet softness. Here you will shed your worries and sit in the shade of the Tree of Life. Here you will join the beat of life and be filled with oneness. Lie down on Earth Mother and put your ear against Her ground. Listen to the movement that travels through Her. Follow Her seasons and hear Her pulse slow with winter and hurry with spring. The spirit of life travels within Her and is born from Her. Ride Her tides of timelessness.

AIR

Come to your quiet place. A stump, a tree to lean against, or a comfortable place on Earth Mother's lap that waits just for you. Look up to Father Sky and Cloud Family. See the clouds. Watch as they race one another. Observe their playfulness. Follow their graceful dance.

Discover cloud embrace. Listen to their song. Feel their spirits touch your eyes and embrace your spirit. Look up with soft eye. Fly with cloud. Know the ecstasy of sky soaring. Time and space will be removed and you will become one with Cousin Cloud.

Come to blue sky. See its vastness. Explore its boundaries. Feel its open arms. Blend in with calm surrender. Time and space will be removed and you will become one with blue sky.

WATER

Come to Cousin Water who teaches the mystery of life. Water teaches us that Gitchi Manidoo is Male, Female and Spirit. It is All. See how frozen water is hard and masculine, how soft and feminine is its liquid, and how vapor transcends this earth into spirit. All in one, one in all, all forms nurture the other. Time and space will be removed and you will become one with ice, water, vapor.

Come to the waterfall for healing. First, sit with your back towards the waterfall. Allow Cousin Water to wash your negative mind and emotions until they are clean and clear. Let waterfall's mist cleanse and empty you. Then turn and face the waterfall. Allow Cousin Water to fill you with positive energies, vibrations, and vapors. Accept the life that Cousin Water gives, for that is its purpose. Water gives its spirits to life.

Come to the shore of a great lake or sea. Sit and watch the waves. Hear the Great Pulse of Life. See how they move in and out, like your breath. Wonder what shores they have touched. Imagine the stories of life they carry. Connect to the possibilities. Follow the movement. Time and space will remove itself and you will become one with Cousin Water.

FIRE

Come to Cousin Fire. Build a fire and watch the flames dance. They will devour time and space and you will enter the Spirit World, the realm of the Eternal. Go back home momentarily and visit your ancestors. Befriend Cousin Fire. See how Cousin has two sides, just as we do. The Bright and the Dark side. The Dark side destroys and devours. The Bright side can blind. Look to the soft light. It illuminates and keeps us warm.

Watch the clouds, watch the waves, and watch the flames. They take you home. They take you to Ain-dah-ing. They take you to your Primary Essence.

Watch the combination of the elements. The sunset's flames ignite the evening clouds. The red, yellow, and purple spirits of the sun trail to the west door of night. Follow the sun trail back home into the Spirit World from which we came. Go home, visit, and experience the celebration. Enlist these powers for they are there to help and guide you. Look and you will see. Listen and you will hear. Touch and you will feel. Do all this with Namaji.

PRAYER STICK

Earth Mother is our connection to Old Age wisdom. Like enlisting Manidoo, the prayer stick becomes our channel to the Spirit World. Just as you became one with the great heartbeat of all, now it is time to sound your heart's intentions.

Find a tree.

As you search, know that Creator decided where the tree should grow. Once you find the tree, thank it for giving you shelter and fuel for your fires. Thank it for giving cool summer shade to rest the Elders and the sleeping child. Thank the tree for giving its branch for birds' nest. Thank the tree for giving its fiery maple leaf to let us know when winter is near. Thank the tree for its running sap that announces spring with its sweet medicine. Thank the tree.

Find your stick. Take a walk around the base of the tree and allow the stick to find you. You will know the stick when you see it, for it will speak to your heart. Once you have found your stick, in a respectful, attentive, way, hug the tree it was once a part of and say a sincere Migwetch to Tree for providing.

You may peel the bark off your stick if you wish and then burn this bark to release its spirits to the Spirit World. This will announce the coming of the prayers you will attach to your prayer stick. Burn sweet grass from the East direction which makes us strong. The sweet grass will thank Brother Tree. Burn tobacco from the South direction, sending your prayers to Father Sky and asking for guidance. Burn sage from the West direction and ask for a cleansing of bad feelings and negative energies. Burn cedar from the North direction to cleanse your mind and heart.

The Four Directions have heard you.

Tie a yellow string on your stick for the East. May your prayer intent be clear and new. May it explode with the wonder of new life.

Tie a red string on your stick for the South. May your prayer intent be of discovery and help you collect your identity. May it move with the energy of youth.

Tie a black string on your stick for the West. May your prayer intent be of Self exploration. May you nurture and grow. May it give you wisdom.

Tie a white string on your stick for the North. May your prayer intent be of connection and completion. May you empty to fill. May you join the Spirit World.

Tie a green string on your stick inward to Earth Mother. May your prayer intent give thanks for Her nurturance and sustenance. May you accept the gifts that are offered.

Tie a blue string on your stick outward to Father Sky. May your prayer intent be of transcendence. May you soar with Brother Eagle and play with Cousin Cloud.

Tie a string of your personal color on your stick to the seventh direction—you. May you become as you are meant to be. May you live your own Bimadisiwin. May you find your Ain-dah-ing.

Embellish your prayer stick as you wish. It is your prayer. Appeal and offer these prayers to the Spirit World.

To activate the prayers, you need to release and engage the stick to the Water Spirits. An ocean, a lake, a river, a stream, or any natural flow of water will send the focused prayers off into the Spirit World. Each prayer will be carried by the spirits of the color of that direction. The prayers of your intent will beat as one.

The Story of Morning Star

Chippewa Lake rippled with little waves, while the sun's glimmer played peek-a-boo in the swollen rice beds. The wild grasses swayed in the summer breeze begging the colored strings of Morning Star's prayer stick to join in their dance. The young woman sat on the sturdy birch branch that extended out from the edge of the lake. She had scooted out as far as was safe, a stick wrapped with colorful strings in her hand, prayers in her heart. Morning Star touched the strings, as her legs dangled over the lake, and thought about her intent, her prayers.

The yellow string was attached for the life that moved inside her. She instinctively rubbed her stomach and looked up into the sky. The young woman prayed for blessing of her baby. Next, Morning Star touched the red string. She thought of the changes she now experienced, the circle of her womanhood, as she nurtured the child within her womb. She asked to be strong, for mornings were difficult to get through. The black string was wrapped around a notch on her stick and Morning Star smoothed out the wrapped string as though comforting a bruise. She asked for wisdom to become a wise mother, to know when to give and when to let go. Morning Star followed the stick's length to its middle, where her mother who was now in the Spirit World, was honored. A tear fell onto the white string washing it with love, as Morning Star imagined her mother's arms around her, proud of the grandchild her daughter now nurtured. Morning Star held the stick up into the wind and let the breeze dry her wet cheeks. She watched the green string dance with the wind. Into the breeze, she thanked Earth Mother for her gifts. The blue string was wrapped for connection. The change in Morning Star's life craved this joining to the Spirit World. Morning Star pulled out an orange string from her pocket. It was for herself. Her becoming. Her being. She wrapped the stick for Morning Star.

The young woman knew it was time to release the prayers to the Spirit World. It was time to give her intent to Gitchi Manidoo. She held it high: her intents, the stick, her prayers. She asked the Seven Directions to take her intents to the Spirit World. Morning Star dropped the stick into the lake and watched as the Wind Spirits carried her intents off into the middle of the lake, until she could no longer see the prayer stick at all.

Three moons passed and Morning Star grew. As her sickness left and she felt alive with great health, the Chippewa River carried her stick along its currents, over rocks, and into still waters. The East and South directions had carried her intent.

Five more moons passed. And Morning Star gave birth to a beautiful boy. Spring turned into Winter and Winter into Spring. Soon he grew into a strong boy. He became known as one who listened more than he spoke, who gave as much as he took, who respected his mother and gave her pride. The Chippewa River had moved West to enter the Great Mississippi. The West direction had carried her intent.

The boy neared adulthood and Morning Star tried to remember what it was like to hold him, where the time had gone. He was still a child, but wore moccasins larger than hers. He was still young, but spoke of adult ways. He was naive, but craved experience. Morning Star needed guidance, as she did not know what to do with her son who was growing so quickly. Morning Star remembered her mother with gentleness and spoke her wise words to her son. The North winds carried Morning Star's prayer further down the great river, and her intent was whirled into the North winds' power.

Her son grew strong and became a great hunter. He brought buffalo back for his people. He fished the waters and harvested the rice. Morning Star's prayers left the shores of Earth Mother and entered the ocean.

Morning Star held her first granddaughter in her arms and smiled at her son. She held responsibility to her people in her arms. She thought of the teachings and the love she would give this fine little one. Father Sky carried her intent out to meet all oceans, where sky blends with water. Morning Star connected to the Spirit World and in turn the Spirit World connected to her people.

Morning Star awoke one night to the sound of the wind. She walked to the lake and leaned against the birch tree where once she had offered her prayers. The woman looked out to the peaceful stillness of the lake. She thought of herself. Her life. Looking up she saw her star and knew the Water Spirits had carried the intent of her prayer stick into the Spirit World, for the wild rice swayed in the light wind and her heart continued to beat the intent of long ago.

With soft step, walk the Red Road of Life. With respect, honor, dignity and pride dance in the Great Circle. Keep your eyes to Sky Father, your feet on Earth Mother, and send your prayers to Gitchi Manidoo. Let the Eagle feather of your heart dignify your gait. Let the Great Drum give cadence to greater Mitakuye-Oyasin. Connect. Become One. Flow with the Great River of Love. Namaji.

CHAPTER 10

THE ARROWS OF CHANGE AND THE SACRED QUIVER

Do not take the Sacred Quiver away,
for it contains his dreams,
her songs
and their dance.

The Arrows of change direct you down the Red Road of Life to help connect you to Gitchi Manidoo, to the Great Love, the Great Mystery. The Arrows are guiding principles, the wisdom of the Great Heartbeat. The Arrows of the Sacred Quiver are made of feathers that ride the winds of the Four Directions. They are honored gifts. They are freeing, rather than restraining. They are WE rather than ME.

The Sacred Quiver contains the Arrows of Change. It is a container made from the fabric of awareness, and is woven from the gifts of Mishomis, Ain-dah-ing, Mash-ka-wisen, Mitakuye-Oyasin, Sacred Hoop, Medicine Wheel, Medicine Bag, Bimadisiwin, and Namaji.

Those who carry the Sacred Quiver next to their hearts, understand that the Arrows help us choose. Our free will acknowledges their power and wisdom. If we chose not to follow their direction, we inflict pain upon ourselves. If we follow the straight course, we fly with the Arrows to reach greater peace, to expand our own Ain-dah-ing. Like the feather lifting the bird to greater heights, the Sacred Quiver and its Arrows lift us into Eternity's current of love.

ARROWS

The Sacred Quiver carries two types of arrows: the Straight and the Crooked. Both arrows represent the movement that is inside each of us as the sun rises and sets. There is movement taking place within us even as we sleep and especially when we dream. Movement is the vehicle for change. There will always be change, either to greater awareness, or deeper denial. Arrows will either strengthen our heartbeat or weaken it.

Arrows have a source and a target. You are the source. You are the bow. The target is either connection or separation: connection to Self and the Spirit World as we separate from life's dramas, or separation from Self and the Spirit World as we connect to life's problems.

I urge you to fill your quiver with straight arrows. Empty your quiver of crooked arrows, as soon as you realize you are carrying them.

The Crooked Arrows

Crooked Arrows can be our teachers if we open our eyes to the target they direct us toward. They teach of consequences. Of pain. They take us off course, as they veer into dark forests of danger.

The Crooked Arrow of Self-Centeredness

Self-centeredness is the inability to go beyond your needs and wants, as well as the inability to laugh at yourself. Those who wear the heavy cloak of life are burdened with the seriousness of Self. Lighten up! Shed yourself and laugh[1]! The Creator must have a very good sense of humor judging by some of His handiwork, including me!

Self-centeredness compensates for a sense of inadequacy[2]. Is there room for fun, humor, or laughter in your life? Or is your walk through life like plodding through slush and sludge? Too much seriousness pulls energy and vision down. People are as unhappy (or as happy) as they want to be. What is your delight? How happy or how unhappy are you? That is the question. You are the answer. Nurture yourself rather than putting demands on others to provide your psychological, emotional, and spiritual nourishment. Claim yourself. Be deliberate in your choice.

<u>*The Crooked Arrow of Fear*</u>

The crooked arrow of anxiety is sharpened with the fear of the future. The arrow of anxiety is fear twisted into the future. Worry can turn into apprehension and panic. The mouse in the closet at night, empowered by fear, gets louder and louder, bigger and bigger, until it has grown into a ferocious bear. The crooked arrow will magnify your fears. Reach within your Medicine Bag for your inner strength. Ward off your fears with Mash-ka-wisen.

<u>*The Crooked Arrow of Dependency*</u>

Vines choke life from Brother Pine. Creeping up the trunks so gracefully, they are cunning and powerful. Beware of attachments. They can squeeze the life out of you. When you become attached, you fail

---

[1] Aristotle once said that the highest state of consciousness is the ability to laugh at oneself.

[2] Egocentrism is a natural developmental stage that all children go through. However, if a child does not receive an adequate amount of attention, affection, recognition and approval from his/her primary caretakers in early childhood, he or she may endlessly try to compensate for this inadequacy by begging, demanding, or searching for it. Many times it is derived from early negative parental messages. It is like having a toothache. You focus on the pain and have a very difficult time enjoying life.

to observe yourself as being independent of people, places, or things. Your identity fuses to another entity. This entity then defines who you are. The tree is no longer simply a tree. It is a host for the vine to crawl on.

Cut yourself loose from the vines that claim you. Grow strong with your own roots. Find the core of who you really are and live with that. Become that. Be that. Let other attachments fall to the ground. Feel the freedom of yourself. Breath fully in knowing you are you. Now you can grow, no longer stifled. Be what life has asked of you.

Consider the young hawk connected to its nest and parents. Each day it is given the food it needs to survive. Each day, its dependency grows as its feathers fill out. Each day it becomes more resistant to leaving the nest. By adolescence, it has grown too big for its nest. The parents know the youngster must leave, but still the young hawk holds on to its familiar life of comfort. It is not willing to take a risk and fly. So the parents do what any good parent must do. They drive the hawk out of the nest and refuse to let it back in. The parents help the hawk break the chains of dependency, so it can soar with the wind and view its own mountain peaks.

Dependencies come in many forms. They are born of fear. From this fear we may become dependent on other people, places, or things. Dependencies may include alcohol, narcotics, food, work, gambling, or sex. People fill their internal voids, their caverns of insufficiencies, with dependencies. They are temporary remedies for what they really need—spiritual sufficiency and balancing.

"Sun-e-gut sheg-a-ba-boo, Sken-a-wa-boo," said Moccasin Mike, warning that beer and whiskey are evil. In spite of his teachings during my adolescence, I became an alcoholic, as do many Indians. Mike, who was otherwise known on Lac Court Orielles Reservation as 'The Lone Ranger'[3], knew that alcoholism would plague his people, as it

---

[3] Mike's white horse, Archie, was the impetus to this nickname.

quickly gave a temporary feeling of sufficiency for a people who had lost so much.

See how the hawk is afraid to fly, and his dependency distracts him from his fear. Recognize how Hawk's hunger pangs paralyze him. Understand that dependencies are driving forces that distract from inner discomfort.

There is an invisible line between water and the ice crystal, just as there is an invisible line between dependencies and addictions. The line is easily crossed from alcohol misuse into alcoholism, from overeating into bulimia, from occasional raffle playing into gambling. When a temporary indulgence turns obsessive and compulsive, when the mind swings to thinking about the substance or object when it should be thinking of other things, when the urge to consume or engage in the substance or experience becomes overwhelming, that is when one is controlled by a dependency.

What would happen if the adolescent hawk was allowed to remain in the nest? There would be greater hunger, greater restlessness, greater pain. Think of the parents. How would they be affected? The dependency of the East, of childhood, *is* necessary to reach the South winds. But let the winds blow through your feathers and flap your wings of freedom. Once we have moved out of the East, we need to become. We can not become if we sit in a nest of dependency. We cannot fly if we are attached to our nest of familiarity. We can never view the mountain if we never take the risk to soar on our own. Just as the hawk must face his fear of independent flight, tap your Mash-ka-wisen, your own inner strength, and face your fear. Respond to the air currents of life and be free.

The Crooked Arrow of Denial

Denial is the delusion of reality. It is the opposite of Mitakuye-Oyasin. When we deny our connectedness to the Universe, we compensate by putting ME above WE. Judgments and comparisons are born from this position.

Judgments are an egocentric condemnation of others for their differences of views, actions, or attitudes. ME is the point of reference, rather than WE. The ME makes the rules to convict. The ME prosecutes and judges. The ME cuts the victim down, in order to gain a false sense of enhancement.

When we focus on differences, rather than similarities, we are at risk for judgmentalism. The "ism" signifies the control judgment holds over us. Judgment spreads like a lightning strike. Don't make others your lightning rod.

Join the Great Circle of Love. Connect to Ain-dah-ing. Share your gifts with those you meet.

Which wave is more important on the ocean? The big wave or the little wave? Comparison is a cousin to judgment. The ME focus of an individual or group defines specific values as absolute. From this judgment is born comparison. This is a black and white system of all or nothing. If you're not with ME, you're automatically against ME. It is a focus on differences rather than on similarities.

These comparisons form camps of self-righteousness and belittlement. If we seek to emphasize our differences, we magnify our separateness and minimize our connectedness. And before you know it, there are just good guys and bad guys. And of course, we (ME) are the good guys and they are the bad guys. We are the ones with the answer sheet to the questions that we wrote!

Consider the idea that just maybe, you and I are both so small and so important at the same time. Today you may be bigger and tomorrow I may tower over you. Today the wave is big, and tomorrow the wave is little. And still each wave is not more important than the other. The big wave and the little wave are one. All are an integral part of the sea. For without the wave, there is no sea. Mitakuye-Oyasin.

The Crooked Arrow of Expectations

If you let the arrows of expectations fly freely, you will be disappointed for they seldom land where you had hoped. If you plan for a sunny day and it rains you will be disappointed. If you plan for a rainy day and it is sunny, you will be disappointed. Expectations are how one person or group thinks another person or group should conduct themselves. What one expects of themselves in terms of beliefs, values, thoughts, philosophies, attitudes, and behaviors is displaced and projected onto others. In other words, what is expected from Self is expected from others. How often have you heard, "How could they do that?"

The expectant person assumes there is only one pair of eyes in the Universe: their own. Many people believe that everyone sees things the same way, and should come to the same conclusions and outcomes. And when something is done that does not match this vision, people react defensively[4]. This reaction may seem justifiable, yet it ends up blocking further connection to Self, others, and ultimately the Spirit World.

This story of identical twins at the seashore illustrates how differently a situation can be experienced:

> Two little boys ran down to the sea to experience the waves. As the ocean retracted, they unknowingly walked into the water's path. And as the ocean returned to the shore, each boy was hit by a large wave and knocked over by its power.

> The first little boy didn't want to get all wet and sandy. He got up quickly, afraid of the power that had hit him. Coughing and spitting, he thought how terrible the water tasted. Afraid, he ran away. Seeing only the shadows, he ran to his mother. Experiencing the wave as hostile, he hated the power of the sea.

---

4 Defense Mechanisms include projecting, minimizing, generalizing, and justifying as a response to defend oneself against a reality that one does not want to accept.

The other twin laughed as he got up from the wet
sand. He liked how his clothes felt, pressed wet
against his warm skin. He smiled at the new
experience of tasting salt water. He was fascinated
by the sea's power. He waited in happy anticipation for the next wave to cover him. He loved the
power of the sea.

Even identical twins don't always see things the same way. It is
easy for us to understand how expectations can interfere with the
small things in life—the likes and dislikes. When I am not like you,
you may become annoyed or disappointed. Even so, it is easier for us
to allow for these small differences than the big differences that make
this world full. The crooked arrow of expectation does not celebrate
our uniqueness—our rich contribution to the Web of Life. Respect
the different values, beliefs, customs, thoughts, philosophies and attitudes of others. Respect the different wave experiences and throw
away your arrows of expectations.

The Crooked Arrow of Stress

Stress originates outside and we bring it inside our Self. We then
tighten up and become rigid. Stress becomes a problem when we are
unable to reverse the process and put it back outside of ourselves
where it belongs. Follow your breath and give tension back to the
world. Grandfather Stone waits to help you give the stress back to the
Water Spirits.

The icy grip of winter puts stress and tension on all of Earth
Mother. She acquiesces to Winter's claim, but she is not claimed. Her
trees yield and the sap sinks down to the roots. Sink down to your
own Ain-dah-ing and yield to the stress of life. Ground yourself to
Earth Mother. Root yourself in Ain-dah-ing. Wear the world like a
loose blanket.

The Crooked Arrow of Depression

Look at Earth Mother. All of Her birds sing! All of Her trees sway! All of Her waters splash! She carries Herself with grace and beauty! She lives with the strong heartbeat of Life!

It is not natural to be depressed. Depression is a sense of feeling helpless, hopeless, afraid, sad, and angry. Depression usually stems from a sense of loss and or a collection of losses[5]. _Depression is the absence of balance. The remedy is the Medicine Wheel._ Balance yourself in all the ways on the Medicine Wheel.

The Arrows in the Flowage
(Part One)

At twelve I thought I knew just about everything.
Living in the forest on Indian Lake with my parents,
I vigorously flapped my wings of independence
each day, fishing, hunting, and traveling the woods.

And I had met Moccasin Mike.

Mike taught me the way of the woods. He would
come to my cabin early in the morning and scratch
on my bedroom screen to awaken me before
daylight. He taught me about the Great Silence
before dawn, as we rowed across the lake to hunt
deer before daybreak. Without words, I learned
lessons of Brother Deer. I learned of Deer's sense
of smell. I learned of Deer's movement. Mike
taught me to count the grains of sand that lifted

---

[5] Depression is paralyzing and psychologically and emotionally painful. Ironically, many people try to escape and avoid depression by ingesting another depressant, alcohol. Truly a paradox. If you drink enough blue dye, you'll probably turn blue. If you drink enough alcohol, you'll probably become depressed.

from Deer's compressed hoof mark in the sand.
From Earth Mother I learned of Deer's visit.

Mike taught me to stand in the pond down the
narrow gravel road and invite the leeches to attach
to my skin. I caught many fish with the leeches.

Mike taught me to listen to the woods. He taught
me many things.

I was a confident young brave. Perhaps, over
confident in the ways of the woods. Yet, Mike had
taught me of Namaji, of Honor, of the Four Directions, of Vision. And I prided myself in listening
well. After all, I could sustain myself for days in
the woods, for all of nature was my companion.

On that summer day of '47, I grabbed my 22-
caliber rifle, bullets, canteen, and jungle hammock
that I had purchased from a U.S. Army Surplus
Store. I said good-bye to my parents and told them
I'd be back in a few days with ducks for dinner. I
decided to go alone to a lake a few miles away. I
left early that afternoon, confident that I would be
at the left end of Green Lake early enough to get
some duck hunting in. As I traveled the deer trails
through the woods, I encountered patches of ripe
blueberries. I could not resist their sweetness.

I went from patch to patch and indulged more and
more, as I wandered further and further from the
deer trail. I was not bending ferns tops, as I was
taught by Mike. As I went through the woods I had
no markers to guide me back to the trail. I drifted
further from high woodlands into lower swamp

lands, farther and farther away from my destination. The shadows crept in while I continued to follow the Blueberry Trail. As night came, I pitched my jungle hammock between two trees. Mosquito netting and rubber-skinned roof were all I needed, I thought, and I curled up in my blanket to doze off with the rain drops hitting my roof.

I awoke the next morning and realized that my selfishness had directed me to the dangerous flowage north and east of Green Lake. The Four Directions I was so proud of knowing, had escaped me. I was lost. Lost in a flowage of floating bogs, prickly brush and muck.

Life suddenly became extremely serious. Anxiety permeated every muscle in my body, as I tightened up trying to make every footstep count. The more I struggled through the swamp, the more the arrow of fear raced through my heart. By the next night lying in my hammock, still nowhere near my destination, I fell asleep wondering what I would do. I was certain no one would find me, for my parents had expected me to be gone for days. That was the way we lived. By the time I fell asleep, I was completely wrapped up in the fear of what the second morning would bring. And in the middle of the night I awoke in stark fear, as a screech owl perched just above me voiced its song. It was the song of my heart.

Walking down the prongs of the flowage, only to find a dead end, I began to feel the pain of another crooked arrow: my dependency. I had been so dependent upon my independent profile, that I had not used the wisdom of Moccasin Mike. I struggled to remember his words, his teachings. I truly needed more than myself. I needed Mike and he was not with me. No longer covered with the vines of self assurance, I stood bewildered before all of nature, alone and afraid. The crooked arrow of dependency had boomeranged on me!

It wasn't long before I struggled against the bog. I did not want to belong to the swamp. I did not want to acknowledge its part in my life. I felt as though Earth Mother was trying to suck me in to join her. I resisted Her. And the more I denied my inevitable connection to Her, the more I was pulled into Her arms.

Yet each moment I expected, I hoped that just around the next corner I would find firm ground once again. But with each moment, it didn't happen. Great despair filled my quiver where the arrow of expectation once rested. By the fifth day, the crooked arrow of stress had made me sluggish. Inevitably, I became the bog. I was the flowage.

By the seventh day, depression had engulfed me. It was all hopeless. I was helpless in the middle of a gigantic flowage. I was scared. I was angry. Losing my reservoir of energy, I had lost all balance. I had lost my Self. At twelve years old, I thought I had lost my life.

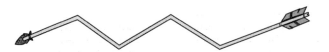

The Straight Arrows of Life

Arrows of straight purpose are made of the strong shafts of Ain-dah-ing. They pierce with sharp tips of awareness, and they fly with the feathers of the Spirit World. Fill your quiver with these straight arrows. They will bring you to the bliss of the Spirit World. With them, you will travel the Sacred Hoop with joy. Following their lead, your life will become the Four Directions.

Come to Self

Pull the first arrow out of your Sacred Quiver. It is the arrow that comes to Self. Travel your path to Self discovery, for you have the ability to observe yourself with your mind's eye[6]. Follow it to the deep pool of Ain-dah-ing. Look into the water's mirror and come to realize your aliveness, your existence, your breath. See your sacred light which permeates from within. Look long and hard at your Self, and discover your life patterns that have become automatic.

In the summer of 1945, there was a long drought in northern Wisconsin. As many lakes dried up I took to walking on the sand bars of the emptied lake bottoms, discovering the hidden world of the lakes I swam and fished. The rains returned, filled their emptiness and I was able to once again swim and fish. Yet the drought changed all future experiences tremendously, for I now knew of the underwater shapes. I now knew of the Great Ice Sheet's carvings and of the deposits of other worlds left behind.

Walk the depths of your unconscious mind. It will forever change your life experiences. Let the rains of new experiences fill up the emptiness. Thank the gifts left behind by the great Ice Sheets of Life. To be aware of Self is to know our depths.

---

[6] The mind's eye is the part of your mind that watches the interaction of all the parts of your mind. The third party observer of our mind, near the center of our forehead, will not allow us to violate our value system while under hypnosis.

Befriend Self

Pull out the second arrow. Its target is friendship of Self. Are you in good or bad company when you are alone? Perhaps the greatest tragedy in life is not befriending yourself. Befriend yourself: your crooked side and your straight side, your bright side and your shadow side. Befriend these sides, for this is the fodder to greater Self experiences. This is the first step. How can you love someone you have not met? The best you can do in that situation is to prize them, for that is the love of the mind. Befriending Self is the first step to Self-Love, the treasure of the heart.

Accept Self

Shoot forth the arrow of Self acceptance. It is an arrow of tremendous energy and guiding wisdom.

Moccasin Mike, with his peg leg and old age, needed the strength and energy of his horse, Archie. Mike gave the horse direction and guided the reigns. As Mike dismounted onto a stump, he'd put a cow bell around Archie's neck. Archie would graze for long summer days and when Mike needed to ride his horse again, he would send me to find him. I would listen for the bell and bring Archie back to Mike. The energy of Archie was free to roam, yet harnessed when needed. Let your energy run, yet bridle it when you must.

Mike is a prime example of Self acceptance. He did not dress for success. He had a couple of shirts, pants, and a jacket. Along with his buckskin, you could probably put all of his clothes in a large gunny sack. He spoke very little English, but fluid Anishinaabe. He probably had enough money hidden in a stump to get a new ax. A very simple life and a very simple existence. Yet he was rich in integrity, friends, animals, and the Universe. But most of all, Mike was Mike and he immensely enjoyed being Mike, even with the loss of a leg and his reservation status. Mike was his own best friend, and why not? Mike will spend eternity with himself and so will you!

Value Self

Feel the feathers of the next straight arrow. Smooth them. This is the arrow of Self-appreciation. Come to value yourself, for you are unique. You are valuable. If you did not exist in the now, the Universe would not be complete. Consider the possibility that if the Universe were not complete, it would cease to exist because it would have an absence. You are that important! Your role on the Sacred Hoop is vitally important. A chaotic ripple effect would vibrate through the Universe and could cause major tears in its fibers. Out of the limitless personages available to experience this now, you have been chosen through the infinite wisdom of Gitchi Manidoo. As the snowflake has its moment in time, so too have you. As a snowflake converts to water and ultimately vapor, so too will you eventually convert back to spirit vapor.

Become Self

When the previous arrows are sharpened, and in your quiver, you are prepared to follow the arrow of Self. With different colors, your arrow flies straight for the target you choose. As a student, a teacher, at church, at Powwow, or as a warrior in the Military, you have become your full Self. Your hats may vary, but your face remains the same. This is a benchmark of actualization. In this process you have become one with Self. This leads you to realize that you and I are one.

Anger, resentment, guilt and remorse freeze the flower in you from blossoming. Ill feelings disconnect you from the Sacred Hoop. Fill up with the waters of Ain-dah-ing and make amends, mending your hoop as you walk your path. Follow your whirlpool of internal currents and tap your Mash-ka-wisen. What may appear difficult is only an exercise in surrendering to the natural process.

Love Self

We spend our entire lifetime in our body day and night, asleep and awake, at home, at work and at play, and for this intimate experience, do we love ourselves? Have we come to see our sacred light? Have we come to Ain-dah-ing?

Find a quiet place, quiet yourself, and talk to yourself as WE. The arrow of love goes straight to your heart and permeates it with a wonderful sense of Self. Pull it out of your quiver and shoot forth this arrow as you love your Self.

Thank your fingers for all they have done to protect and sustain you. Thank your toes and your feet for having born your weight and carried you great distances down your path of life. Thank your heart, your life drum, for maintaining a constant beat that pumps your blood throughout your body. Thank your arteries and veins for being the rivers and streams within that carry nourishment and breath to all your internal encampments. Thank your nose for bringing you all those pleasurable scents that are found in the forest. Thank your eyes for beholding the beauty of the sunset. Thank your skin for being your rain coat in the storm and your blanket in the wind. Thank your ears for allowing you to hear the symphony of the Universe. And thank your tongue for the experience of a parched throat embracing a cool fresh drink of water, the beverage of the Creator.

Hear this Anishinaabe Prayer:

> How then can I tell you of my love?
> Strong as the Eagle, Soft as the Dove.
> Patient as the Pine Tree that stands in the sun.
> And whispers to the wind, "You are the One."

Being of love essence, you will blossom into yourself: a love reflection of the Creator.

Celebrate Self

With great joy, pull out your arrow of Self celebration. Be glad for what you have accomplished, be glad for what the world has accomplished. The first questions the Creator might ask us when we return home to the Spirit World is, "Did you enjoy my creation? Did you bask in the sun? Did you listen to the bird singers? Did you smell Sister Cedar's perfume? Did you see the glistening dew polish Cousin Fern? Did you taste the fruit of the forest?"

Look to Life to provide joy and happiness and wear the joy well with your laugh and smile lines. The most precious gift given me was from my mother. She taught me to enjoy the moment, enjoy the experience, and to carry those memories in my facial expressions and joy lines. We can tell how a person chooses to live life from their countenance. Your face is the billboard of your lifestyle.

Wherever I go, I am probably there with a smile on my face. How good it feels! Indians laugh a lot. Some laugh so hard that the chair they sit in shakes like a wet dog. Seek these moments out. Look for humor. It is there. Humor is no more than contradiction, and life is filled with it!

One spring day I was sitting in my boat fishing for walleyes. I was watching another person in his boat, pounding posts in the lake bottom by the shoreline to support a pier. As I watched him pound with a sledge hammer, he missed the post, but hung onto the sledgehammer handle and followed it head first into the lake. Well, that made my day on the reservation, fish or no fish! I can't remember what I caught that day, but the image still tickles me. I have to give him credit, for he went right back to swinging that hammer. If he was a fun seeker, he was able to laugh at himself and is still savoring the memory of that day.

We are here for such a short time, so enjoy the experience. Enjoy your Self.

Share Self

The last arrow is the one that must be shared. Give it now, freely.

Look to and learn from the robin. How stately, how unpretentious, how humble, how predictable, how friendly. The robin is a good model for us. It gives itself easily to all the world.

Give your time, your Self, to others. Help with a door, slow down for the aged, read to a child. Give your best. Share your smiles. Share your joy as well as your sadness. Serve others to serve yourself. To give is a basic need. That is integrity. If you think you are humble, you probably are not. If you think you are not humble, you probably are.

Practice humility. Humility opens the door to patience. Practice patience, for patience opens to tolerance. Practice tolerance. Tolerance opens the door to compassion. Practice compassion for it swings back open to humility. Practice all of these aspects of Self and you will find integrity. Reach within yourself to enrich society. Enrich society and you will enrich yourself.

The Arrows in the Flowage
(Part Two)

Then something happened.

In the middle of my despair, in the middle of my self-inflicted pain, the Spirit World participated in my journey to Self.

On the eight day, when my canteen was long empty and my stomach pains begged me to eat something other than the plentiful berries, when I had lost my vision of home, Mu-kwa'[7] was sent for me to see. He was running so fast through the flowage that he appeared to be skipping across the rippling bog.

That visit from Mu-kwa' shot my first straight arrow. I finally came to Self and observed myself from above. I saw a brave fighting his way against nature, rather than going with nature. I

---

7 Mu-kwa' means bear in Anishinaabe.

saw reactions rather than responses. I saw a brave who needed to sustain himself in order to save himself.

I looked around and realized that nature hadn't changed. I had changed. Mother Earth waited to give me her gifts of food. All I had to do was to look for the nourishment that was always there. I began to remember the words of Mike. I recalled that a poplar sapling was a source of nourishment. I cut it down and peeled back its bark and thanked it for its sweet juicy meat.

Soon, I shot a porcupine and a squirrel. I thanked them for giving me their life, in order for me to live. I caught the rain from Cousin Clouds in a birch bark bucket and filled my canteen.

I heard Moccasin Mike tell me that I could either be my best friend or my worst enemy. What would it be? I dug deep into my own Mash-ka-wisen and became the best that I could be in the swamp. For the swamp was now my life. It was all that was there. What is, is. I had a choice to embrace it or fight it. Remembering Mu-kwa', I saw that the impossible could become possible.

I replayed the memory of Bear crossing the bog. How did he do it? What was the secret? My only chance at survival was to cross the prongs of land that separated the bog's treacherous middle. I had to become Brother Mu-kwa' and skip across with grace and countenance.

The Spirit World guided me in discovering the truth. It was all about balance. Like the Medicine Wheel, Mu-kwa' distributed his weight in order to maintain his balance on the dangerous floating bogs. His balance was a precise blend of all Four Directions, his four paws giving him the gift of equal distribution.

So I became Mu-kwa' with the help of Earth Mother. I wove saplings together to form three 6' by 4' rectangles. I tied them together with the leathery fibers of moose hide plant. I peeled back Sister Cedar's bark to find the layer just inside. By soaking those fibers and tying the saplings together while the cedar fibers were still wet, the fibers dried into a very strong twine. I had flat beds to distribute my weight to the Four Directions. I would cross as Brother Mu-kwa' had.

I crossed the bogs with great care. I placed one of my flats beside the one I was on, to carry my supplies. Then I moved the flat that was behind me in front to become a flat for me to crawl onto. Inch by inch, I moved forward. The flat with my supplies moved as I moved, alongside me. In this way I began to cross the flowage, balancing my weight to all Four Directions.

During the long hours of half crawling, half slithering, I became thankful of the strength in my arms. I thanked them for their help. I thanked my feet for getting me as far as they had. In the long hours of quiet night, I thanked Mu-kwa' for teaching me about balance.

After sleeping that night on the flowage bog, a day and a half after beginning this bear crawl, I reached my vision of land. Solid land.

I shouted with joy for all of nature to hear as I recognized the woods. I had come out at Chief Lake, ten days after my departure from home, six miles off course.

My heart beats strong as I remember this journey to Self. It is the heartbeat of my ancestors. It is the same beat of your heart.

THE SACRED QUIVER

Honor

You bring honor to yourself and to all your relations by carrying your Sacred Quiver with you wherever you go. Honor the Earth and Her inhabitants. The Sacred Quiver is made of commitment, responsibility, and accountability. Ultimately, we need only to answer to ourselves and our Creator. But our challenge is to put our greed and selfishness aside to accommodate the WE, not the ME. When the natural order is disturbed, it comes back to haunt us personally, socially, and it affects the Universe. Therefore, honor the Earth and respect all things.

Soft and Hard Eyes

The Sacred Quiver is both hard and soft. The individual fibers are soft, yet when they come together, they become hard. The soft or feminine energy is creativity. The hard or masculine energy is conceptual. Think of the male seed that initiates life. Think of the female womb that gives life. Both are needed in order for life to advance.

Woman has within her the soft secret of creation, as all things are born from her. She is the center of society. Yet, man supports woman's nurturing. Soft focus in both men and women is the creativity of the Universe. On the Medicine Wheel of life cycles, male grows older and becomes more female by losing hair and becoming more gentle. Female becomes more male by growing hair and becoming more forceful. These internal shifts are nature's way of bringing us to balance. The male's hard conceptive seed pierces the soft female egg, just as Acorn pierces Mother Earth. When these two energies combine, the two produce the One. Light masculine energy precedes from the darkness of feminine energy. What is emptied (the womb) is filled, and what is filled (pregnancy) is emptied (birth). We are to experience birth energies. It is both the female and the male, the creativity and the conceptual, the nurturing and the supportive, the hard and the soft. It is all of procreation. It is all of life. It is all Sacred.

See with soft focus. Create and nurture. See the Spirit World with soft eyes and give it form.

See with hard focus. Initiate and support. See the Natural World with hard eyes and give it honor.

Vision

The Sacred Quiver has a purpose, a vision for the arrows it contains. Only the person carrying the Quiver knows of the purpose, knows of the vision. It is the sacred right of the traveler to follow his own vision, to follow her path on the Sacred Hoop of Life. Do not take the Sacred Quiver away from him, for it contains his dreams, her songs and their dance. Do not discount the size of his quiver, for you do not know the threads that it is made of.

Bring your dream, your song, and your dancer together and sing the dream-dance of life as you wear your quiver close to your heart.

Wear bells and jingles and celebrate life movements. Let the jingles encourage the spirits to dance with you, especially your spiritual animal affinity.

In a morning conversation with my friend, Aught Coyhis, we discussed personal vision. Aught's seventy-two years have given him many dreams to dance. As a Mohican and Oneida-Iroquois, he is a former tribal chairman of the Stockbridge-Munsee tribe and worked very hard to make his vision for his Nation come true. In the early 1970's, Aught went to Washington D.C. to watch President Nixon sign a land bill that increased the area of his reservation by 13,077 acres. That was one of Aught's dreams. And he danced it well. His dance is a remarkable legacy for his grandchildren.

Aught spoke of other visions. He spoke of respect. He spoke of simplifying and cultivating our spiritual lives. He spoke of the minority becoming the majority, for that is the natural order of things. He spoke of understanding, as brothers and sisters of other nations, colors, and persuasions join hands.

Listen to Aught's heart. It beats a strong message for our future.

Listen to your own heart. It beats its own strong message. We all need to come to our own Bimadisiwin. Live your full life and cultivate your personal vision. Personal vision is the vision for all.

Feel the fabric of the Sacred Quiver. With your Spiritual touch, follow its threads of truth. Understand the pain and joy of the thousands of years that went into making this container for you. Thank the Great Spirit for its making. Woven together, the strands are the binding, strong support for life choices. Shoot forth the straight arrows of healing. Hear the Great Heartbeat that the Sacred Quiver rests against. It is the Heartbeat of One.

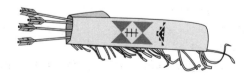

PART FIVE

THE DRUM SPEAKS

Hear this prayer read at Indian
Alcoholics Anonymous meetings:

O Great Spirit,
whose voice I hear in the winds,
and whose breath gives life to all the world,
hear me! I am small and weak.
I need your strength and wisdom.

Let me walk in beauty and make my eyes ever behold
the red and purple sunset.
Make my hands respect the things you have made
and my ears sharp to hear your voice.
Make me wise so that I may understand
the things you have taught my people.
Let me learn the lessons you have hidden
in every leaf and rock.

I seek strength
Not to be greater than my brother,
but to fight my greatest enemy—myself.
Make me always ready to come
to you with clean hands and straight eyes,
so when life fades, as the fading sunset,
my spirit may come to you without shame.

Mitakuye-Oyasin

CONCLUSION

Listen to the voice of the Great Spirit
In your Heartbeat.
Come to the center of your existence
and Listen.

Listen to the drum.

The drum will teach you, tell you, show you, help you. A mother's heartbeat is a song to her child, connecting her child to the outside world. You are Earth Mother's child. Hear Her vibration and connect to Her Pulse, for the Drum speaks through Her to those who listen. Remember the lessons of eagle and rock, of pine and cloud. Take your place on the Sacred Hoop and listen to the silence within. Each beat is a reminder of both, the natural and the spiritual dimensions.

The drum beats.

Hear the water drum's soft beat. Hear the strong beat of Pow-wow. Sound your own distinct drum and join the Great Pulse of all.

No drum is too small, no beat is too soft. All contribute. Participate joyfully with the great vibration of the Universe. Dance to your own rhythm and celebrate your life.

LEARN FROM THE DRUM

It beats in the Now, with the steady full beat of Life. Live with that same pulse.

Don't worry, don't hurry, do your best, and forget the rest!

The Drum is steady, always in the Now, as each beat is as important as the one before and the one to follow. The present is your vital opportunity. It is where you live. Worry is fear of the future. Worry is like taking a blank sheet of paper, placing it on your mind's easel, and drawing a horrible fairy tale. Your animated horror is viewed by your mind's eye and causes panic. Unable to distinguish between pretend and real, you become the victim of your own terrorism. Worry is ineffective. Worry consumes the power of each moment. Possibilities are devoured by fear.

If you must paint mental pictures, paint positive ones. Soothe your mind's eye with beauty, and relax. Since all worry, all fear, is in the future, all you need to do is switch back to the present. If you find yourself in future, turn off the worry light switch and live in the Now.

The Great Mystery is steady and maintains the beat of Life. There is no rush. Each moment is important and worthy of a full pulse. Be steady. Don't hurry. You were not made to hurry. Hurry is an effort to distract from Self. Distraction prevents Self from experiencing Self, which prevents you from accessing your Ain-dah-ing. Your home within your heart houses your tranquillity.

The more you hurry, the further away you get from home and the more you become fixed on external events, leaving an internal emptiness. If this emptiness is not filled internally by your spirituality, it will seek fulfillment with external stimulation. The door is left wide open for addiction, or the erosion of identity. The next thing you know, you are looking for Self in the quality of your wristwatch or automobile. You become a temporal being rather than the spiritual being you are. You are back to being a body with a spirit, rather than your true essence—a spirit with a body.

Things start to go so fast in distraction, they begin to control you and you lose your grip. You lose inner control of Self. You start to ask yourself, "Why did I do that? Why can't I stop doing that? Why do I feel so bored and empty?" Slow down. Come to Self. Come to Ain-dah-ing. Drink the sweet waters of your inner spring.

The beat of the Universe is full and fills its container, Earth Mother, with the vibrations of life. Likewise, be full. Live fully. Do your best. Live your Bimadisiwin. Old Age wisdom was taught by the tribe, band, clan, and Elders as they instilled Bimadisiwin. The dignity of living life fully is implicit in Namaji. It is not a competitive best among others. It is a competitive best with yourself. Be who you are. Be you. You as you are. Bring your uniqueness to your people.

In the sacred Midewinin[1] Eagle Medicine Lodge, the Medicine Man makes an apparent mistake in his elaborate bead work in order to announce his humanity. This obvious mistake reveals that all are flawed, no one is exempt. All bring their distinct Self to the Council Circle. Some are strong, some are weak, some older, some younger, some feminine, some male, some shy, some bold. Don't be fooled by profile or posture.

The small badger ferociously stands his ground, undefeated by the most vicious aggressor on the continent, the wolverine. The badger is smaller, but his center of gravity is low. The wolverine cannot defeat the badger, despite his boasts of dominance. Likewise, the lynx who is much smaller than his cousin cougar, drives the cougar from his high mountain territory to the lower elevations because the cougar is vulnerable to the lynx's low attack.

You, too, have your unique strengths. Tap into your Mash-ka-wisen and come to Self. You, too, are not as vulnerable as you might

---

[1] Midewinin is pronounced: mi-Day-win and means the sacred medicine lodge of the Ojibway people.

think. Lower your center of gravity and connect to Earth Mother, the Spirit World, and the Medicine Wheel. Balance. Do your best and you will have done your best.

The Big Drum beats of life. Do the same, dance to your own life and forget the rest. Let go of trying to control people, places and things. You can't anyway, so why try? There is only one thing you can control in the Universe, and that is your Self. That is why you need to control yourself. Forget trying to control nature, that's the Creator's job. Be content to live just your life and live your life to the fullest. Let your life flow like the sugar maple tree in spring. Don't hang onto the bitterness. Anger, resentment, guilt and remorse will devour you. Let them go, give them up, their thorns and their pain. The pain will become your obsession, as the porcupine quill in the nose of the bear, and will separate you from your brothers, sisters and cousins. This self-inflicted pain sinks like a saturated log in a lake. Let go, or these negatives will pull you down into the muck of life. Lift your head. Look up. Respect all. Fear none. And let the Spirit World take care of the rest.

MAKE WISE DECISIONS

A few years before I came from the Spirit World my parents chose where to build our home on the reservation. They chose a piece of land that was at one time a small island in the lake. It had lodged itself to the shoreline and consequently, the roots of the trees had bound to the main land. Driving the point of a well-tip into the sand with a sledge hammer, my dad successfully accessed a spring at seventeen feet deep.

Then my father made a very wise decision. This well-spring became the center of our home. He built our home with the help my great uncle and grandfather. He built the kitchen sink adjacent to the pump handle, which was now inside the kitchen. Even without electricity, we didn't have to go outside in the rain or cold to tap our life sustaining water-source.

Build your life around your inner center of existence, which supplies your life force and energizes your spirit. Build your home within your heart—your Ain-dah-ing—over your spiritual well-spring, so you, too, can tap your Mash-ka-wisen without difficulty.

Find your well-spring. Accommodate your life around it. Build your home within your heart over its center. Nurture your Self as a spirit with a body. Nourish your spirit, so that your body, mind, and emotions can trail with Namaji. Live, let live, and celebrate life.

Make wise decisions based on seven generations. Think how your decisions will directly affect the next generations. Take your responsibility seriously, and make every decision and behavior reflect your commitment to living in harmony and in the best interest of Earth Mother and Sky Father. Your children and all life forms require your greatest Namaji, because they are relying on you to love and care for life.

Bless the Children.

BLESS THE CHILDREN

Children are the fabric of our future. Honor them. Do nothing which shall harm them. This includes all children, the child within oneself, others, and the children of the Earth and Sky. We need to honor the Earth and see how delicate all species are. If we live in harmony with the child of All, the sky is clear, the earth is solid. All is content, flourishes, and the sacred cycle renews. Honoring the children ensures the continuance of the male and female energies. When the child within all is abused, the sky becomes dirty, and the earth barren. Balance is lost and creatures disappear forever.

Your greatest treasure is your child within. Continue to nurture your child even as you grow old. The child is forever part of you. The child-within gifts you the freedom that you crave, the spontaneity you wish for, the wonder you desire. Go to the East direction when in need of these things. Remain connected to your child.

Go to a petting zoo and watch the children of all colors admire one another. The humans admire the ducklings, lambs, colts, calves, chicks, piglets, kittens and puppies. These children of the Earth admire the human children and come back for an endless amount of affection. This continues until all are so exhausted from this exchange, they collapse into slumber. This illustrates the pure quality of mutual respect. This respect is the ebb and tide of the Universe. Bear cub, wolf cub and cougar cub all play together, for they see their similarities, not differences. They see cub. See with child eyes and you, too, will always see your affinity with all of life.

Children are our riches. Like a beautiful stone with many facets, view the children in different lights. Allow them the freedom to be a child, yet bless them with limits and boundaries, too. For that is the nourishment of their shell. If we do not nourish them with definition in childhood, they will impose many on themselves in adulthood. To honor our children is to provide them with both sunlight and shadows.

THE RIVER OF LIFE

We are all moving along the River of Life. Enjoy the scenery. Look and you will see the Creator. Fish along the way and play. Pull your canoe up on the shoreline and rest. Pick berries and collect them in your birch bark basket. Enjoy their bitter-sweetness. Taste the blueberry, and you will taste the Creator. Build a nice fire and cook your fish. Taste the fish and you will taste the Creator. Place tobacco down and thank the Four Directions for their gifts. Burn sage, sweet grass, and cedar. You will smell the Creator. Watch the sun trail to the West. It is the glory of the Creator. Tell your companions of your journey and listen to theirs. Tell stories around the fire and enjoy each other's company. Tell jokes. Laugh. Enjoy. Look into the eternal of Cousin Fire and you will touch the Creator's Pulse. Rest under Grandmother Moon's gaze and sleep well.

Realize that all rivers lead to the ocean. All streams lead to the Creator. Mitakuye Oyasin. We are all related.

LISTEN WITH A SHARP EAR

Prayer is talking to the Creator

Pray with your internal water drum to the Spirit World. You are two-thirds water and one-third earth. The water drum represents the merging of Earth and the spiritual dimensions. Send your drum beat to the Creator from your water drum.

Approach prayer humbly. Humility is recognizing your sacred role. Prayer is the key to opening Self. When you open to the Spirit World, you open Self so that you can fulfill yourself with spiritual peace and joy. Someone said to me, "If you pray, don't worry. And if you worry, don't pray." They don't mix. Have faith in the one you love and the one who loves you—the Creator.

Pray with intent and with accuracy. Engage your gifts of Ain-dahing; be open, honest, calm, direct, and clear. For "your tongue is to speak with when you know what to say and how to say it. Your teeth are to keep your tongue in your mouth until you figure it out." May your prayers be of all directions and may the seventh direction reflect the color of yourself. May your prayers fly on the wings of Brother Eagle.

Connect the invisible with the visible. Burn sweet grass, tobacco, sage, cedar, and kinnikinnick to open the channels to the Spirit World.

Call the Spirits with these powers and they will come. Pray from your heart.

Meditation is listening to the Creator.

Meditation begins where thought ends. This is the cradle board, the pouch, the threshold, the womb of the Great Mystery.

To hear the spiritual whispers of the Drum, find yourself a sacred place, a place that is different than your ordinary realm; a stump or rock in the woods. Listen to the unseen voices: peepers in the spring, birds high above, snapping twigs, Brother Chipmunk.

If this is not within your reach, go to the eternal blessing of Sky family. Look up to Grandfather Sun, Grandmother Moon, Cousin Cloud and all the Star people who are singing and dancing the song of the Universe. Embrace them and they will speak to your heart. The Sky Drum resonates throughout the Universe for those who listen. The Sky Drum's vibrations makes the stars flicker and cause Grandmother Moon to cast Her shadow down on the great waters, making the tides flow. Dance to Sky Drum and you will celebrate with the Night Singers. Join Brother Wolf and Sister Whippoorwill as they provide a chorus from here below. Come to know that as you look up with celestial appreciation, Sky family happily looks down as Grandparents watch their grandchildren dance and frolic. The old need the young and the young need the old. Sky needs you, as you need the Sky. Mitakuye-Oyasin.

Find your quiet place. Sit comfortably. Relax. Mentally collapse. Follow your breath and connect with all of your visible companions on Earth Mother. Follow your breath and connect to the invisible.

In your home within your heart, rest. In the pause between the beat of life, listen.

Learn from Turtle. Turtle comes out of the water realm to rest on a log and bask in Grandfather Sun's rays and Grandmother Moon's light. It stops its life, quiets, and sheds the leeches that cling to its shell. Shed your stressors and tensions that cling to your shell. Stop your life, quiet to meditation, and open up to the Great Spirit's White Light.

You need to listen with a sharp ear to the silent voice of the Spirit World. Quiet the noise of your Self and rest your head on the pillow of life. Listen and you will hear the Great Pulse of the Creator.

Take the moment, Now, and celebrate your own mystery by exploring your inward spiritual caves and caverns. Find yourself, Now, in the going and returning of your breath, as you follow it to guide you through your internal expedition. Come to the center of your existence, Now, your well-spring within, where the voices of your Grandfathers and Grandmothers murmur. This is the center of your heart, the alignment of your mind, body, and spirit. It is the space between the tricksters of desire and fear. Here you will not be distracted from Self. Listen to the voice of the Great Spirit in your spiritual heartbeat. Come to the center of your existence, to your Primary Essence, and listen.

Listen to the Drum.

> The song of the drum filled the round house lodge, and around its edges sat all of the Elders. I looked around and saw that the Elders' smiles were all wrapped in Grandfather Sun's light, as was this August evening. Thinking about what I would say to them about alcoholism, I sat in my place of the circle, wrapped in my own sunlight of honor.

> But before the teaching would begin, a familiar Elder asked me to assist him in building the ceremonial sacred fire. I eagerly got up to participate in this privilege.

> The sacred fire circle waited, and soon I was busy chopping and splitting wood. Throughout the preparation of the fire, this man of many moons

prayed vigorously in his Potawatomi tongue. I
moved the firewood around to encourage the
marriage of fire and air, and I listened to his prayer.
With a spirited beat, he prayed. Like the constant
waves of the sea, his prayer moved.

All the while, I listened. All the while, I tended the
sacred fire. All the while, he prayed.

He reached into his Medicine Bag and sprinkled
some kinnikinnick over the fire. Releasing its
spirits, he continued to pray. His voice became
stronger.

Suddenly, the blind man paused in the midst of his
prayer and said to me, "Look up. Are they here
yet?"

Nearing ninety, his excitement could not wait for
my response and again he asked, "Are they here
yet?"

My eyes followed the sacred smoke trail into Sky
Father. I watched as four eagles flew in from each
direction. Soaring on Cousin Wind, they neared
each other. Meeting as brothers, the eagles became
a great hoop above us. And connecting to the beat
of the eternal, I said, "Ah ho."

GLOSSARY

Word	Pronunciation	Definition
Ain-dah-ing	AH-da-ning	Home. Referred to as home within our heart.
Anishinaabe	a-ni-shi-NA-bae	Those who were the ancestors of the tribes now known as Ottawa, Potawatomi, and Ojibway.
Bimadisiwin	be-ma-DEE-zee-win	To live life to the fullest. To become and fulfill one's fate and purpose. To engage free will. Sometimes spoken by Elders to mean: to live the good life.
Boo-zhoo	Bou-zshoo	Hello.
Cedar medicine		Used in many spiritual ceremonies to provide a channel to the Spirit World.
Crooked Arrows		Arrows that warn of life strategies that will bring you to greater pain.
Eagle Medicine Feather		Known in Ojibwa tradition to be used in healings.
Earth Mother		Recognizing the female, creative, nurturing qualities of the earth.
Four Directions		The Four Directions of the Medicine Wheel: East, South, West, and North.

Word	*Pronunciation*	*Definition*
Gee'-sis	GEE-sis	The Sun, which is Grandfather.
Gitchi	GI-chi	Great.
Gitchi Manidoo	GI-chi MON-ee-doo	Great Spirit.
Gitchi Migwetch	GI-chi ME-gwich	Big thank you.
Kinnikinnick	KIN-ee-kin-ik	"Much mixed." Is a tobacco based mixture also accompanied with other herbs, primarily: cedar, balsam fir, sweet grass, calamus root, sweet non-fern, sweet gale and mints. Other mixtures may also include bear berry, sweet goldenrod, rose petals, sage, willow bark, red ooshier bark, sweet clover yarrow and tobacco. Used in Native American sacred ceremonies.
Manidoo	MON-ee-doo	Spirit.
Mash-ka-wisen	mash-KOW-sin	Inner strength.
Medicine Bag		A Native American healing pouch that contains a variety of herbs, medicines etc. used to connect to the participant to the Spiritual Realm.
Medicine Wheel		A Native American healing wheel to represent balance in one's life, as well as a symbol for life cycles. The Medicine Wheel has three parts: the circumference (the Sacred Hoop), the center (Gitchi Manidoo), and the Four Directions (East, South, West, and North).

Word	Pronunciation	Definition
Michi-Gami	MICH-ee-GAM-ee	Great water. The root word of Michigan.
Midewinin	mi-DAY-win	Sacred Medicine Lodge of the Ojibway people.
Migwetch	ME-gwich	Thank you.
Mishomis	mi-SHOO-mis	Grandfather in the Ojibway language. Is also a term for the spiritual healing stone.
Mitakuye-Oyasin	mi-TAHK-wee-a-say	We are all related.
Mu-kwa	MA-kwa	Bear.
Namaji	NA-MA-GEE	The highest Anishinaabe principle: respect, honor, dignity and pride.
Nee-ba-gee'-sis	NEE-ba-GEE-sis	The Moon, which is Grandmother.
Nokomis	no-KO-mis	Grandmother.
Oon-da'-di-zoo-win'	ON-da-DEE-zoe-win	Birth.
Prayer Stick		A way to lift your prayers to the Great Spirit.
Red Road		The guiding principle to stay between virtue and evil, to have a positive focus.
Sacred Hoop		A Native American symbol for our journey in this life, as well as our connection to the Spirit World. It also illustrates the cycle of all things.
Sacred Quiver		A term to symbolize the carrying of sacred arrows (guiding principles) to live by.

Word	*Pronunciation*	*Definition*
Sahgeen	San-GEEN	Love and respect.
Seven Directions		Represents the seven directions for one's life: East to the eagle, South to the wolf, West to the buffalo, and North to the bear, in to Earth Mother, out to Sky Father and yourself—the seventh direction.
Shapeshift		A cognitive reframing.
Sky Father		Recognizing the conceptual, supportive qualities of Sky.
Straight Arrows		Principles that will bring you to greater health and connection with the Universe.
Vision Quest		A Native American ceremony where the participant abstains from food, light, etc. in order to obtain a spiritual vision to guide his free will in directing his purpose. Sometimes conducted in pits, mountain tops, or near a waterfall.

INDEX

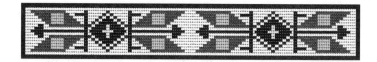

SUGGESTED READING

Alcoholics Anonymous: Big Book (3rd Ed.). New York: Alcoholics Anonymous World Services, Inc., 1976.

Benton-Banai, Edward. *The Mishomis Book: The Voice of the Ojibway.* Saint Paul, MN: Red School House, 1988.

Campbell, Joseph. *The Hero With a Thousand Faces.* (3rd Ed.). New York: Bollingen Foundation Inc., 1973.

Erdoes, Richard & Ortiz, Alfonso, (Eds.). *American Indian Myths and Legends.* New York: Pantheon Books, 1984.

Freesoul, John Redtail. *Breath of the Invisible: The Way of the Pipe.* Wheaton, Ill: The Theosophical Publishing House, 1986.

Gibran, Kahlil. *The Prophet.* New York: Alfred A. Knopf, 1968.

James, Wharton. *Learning from the Indians, 1908.* Philadelphia: Running Press, 1973.

Kelsey, Morton. *Dreamquest: Native American Myth and the Recovery of Soul.* Rockport, MA: Element, 1992.

McClellan, Marian A. *Seeds of Stillness: Opening to the Self.* Santa Barbara: Fithian Press, 1994.

Ross, A.C. *Mitakuye Oyasin: "We are all Related".* Kyle, SD: Bear, 1989.

Summers, Caryn L. *The Girl, The Rock & The Water: Rediscovering the Child Within.* Salt Lake City, UT: Commune-A-Key Publishing, 1994.

Sweet, Denise. *Days of Obsidian, Days of Grace.* Duluth, MN: Poetry Harbor, 1994.

The Sacred Tree: Reflections on Native American Spirituality. Lethbridge, Alberta, Canada: Four Worlds Development Press, 1984.

Walker, Deward E., Jr. *Myths of Idaho Indians.* Moscow, ID: University of Idaho Press, 1980.

ABOUT THE AUTHORS

Muka-day-way-ma-en'-gun, Blackwolf, is the Indian name given to co-author Robert Jones. He is of Ojibway heritage and lived on the Lac Courte Oreilles-Ojibway reservation during his formative years. Blackwolf frequently visits his home to renew and further the Anishinaabe way.

Blackwolf achieved sobriety in 1977 within the fellowship of Alcoholics Anonymous and has enjoyed continuous sobriety since that time. He holds a Bachelor's degree in Psychology, a Master's degree in Guidance and Counseling and has accomplished post graduate studies in Addictive Disorders. He is a licensed psychotherapist, a Certified Addiction Specialist, and has published in an international professional journal. He maintains a private clinical practice and speaks nationally about Native American healing techniques within the psychotherapeutic process.

Gina Jones is of Mohawk ancestry. She, too, has enjoyed continuous sobriety since 1979. Holding a Bachelor's of Science degree in Education, Gina is presently a sixth grade teacher. She presents inservice training on Reading and Writing Workshops for educators in Wisconsin.

Gina writes in her free time on her own projects, as well as in conjunction with her husband. She has published curriculum material through CESA (Cooperative Educational Service Agency) in Wisconsin, poetry in literary publications, and is currently looking forward to publishing other material, including children's books and young adult novels.

COMMUNE-A-KEY PUBLISHING AND SEMINARS

Commune-A-Key Publishing and Seminars, Inc. was established in 1992. Our mission statement, "Communicating keys to growth and empowerment," describes our endeavor to publish books that inspire and promote personal growth and wellness. Our goal is to discover and develop *products that heal.* All of our books and products provide powerful ways to care for, discover and and heal ourselves and others.

Our audience includes health care professionals and counselors, caregivers, men, women, people interested in Native American traditions, adolescents—anyone interested in personal growth, recovery and inspiration. We hope you enjoy this book. If you have comments, questions, or would like to be on our mailing list for future products and seminars, please send them on to us at:

Commune-A-Key Publishing
P.O. Box 58637
Salt Lake City, UT 84158

Migwetch!